W9-BLV-438

The Merrill Spelling Program

Spelling for Writing

Robert L. Hillerich
Sharon Gould

Charles E. Merrill Publishing Co.
A Bell & Howell Company

Acknowledgment

The riddle headings used in this book are taken from *1001 Riddles for Children* by George Carlson. Copyright © 1949 by Platt & Munk Publishers. Reprinted by permission.

ISBN 0-675-04414-6

Published by
Charles E. Merrill Publishing Co.
A Bell & Howell Company
Columbus, Ohio 43216

Printed in the United States of America

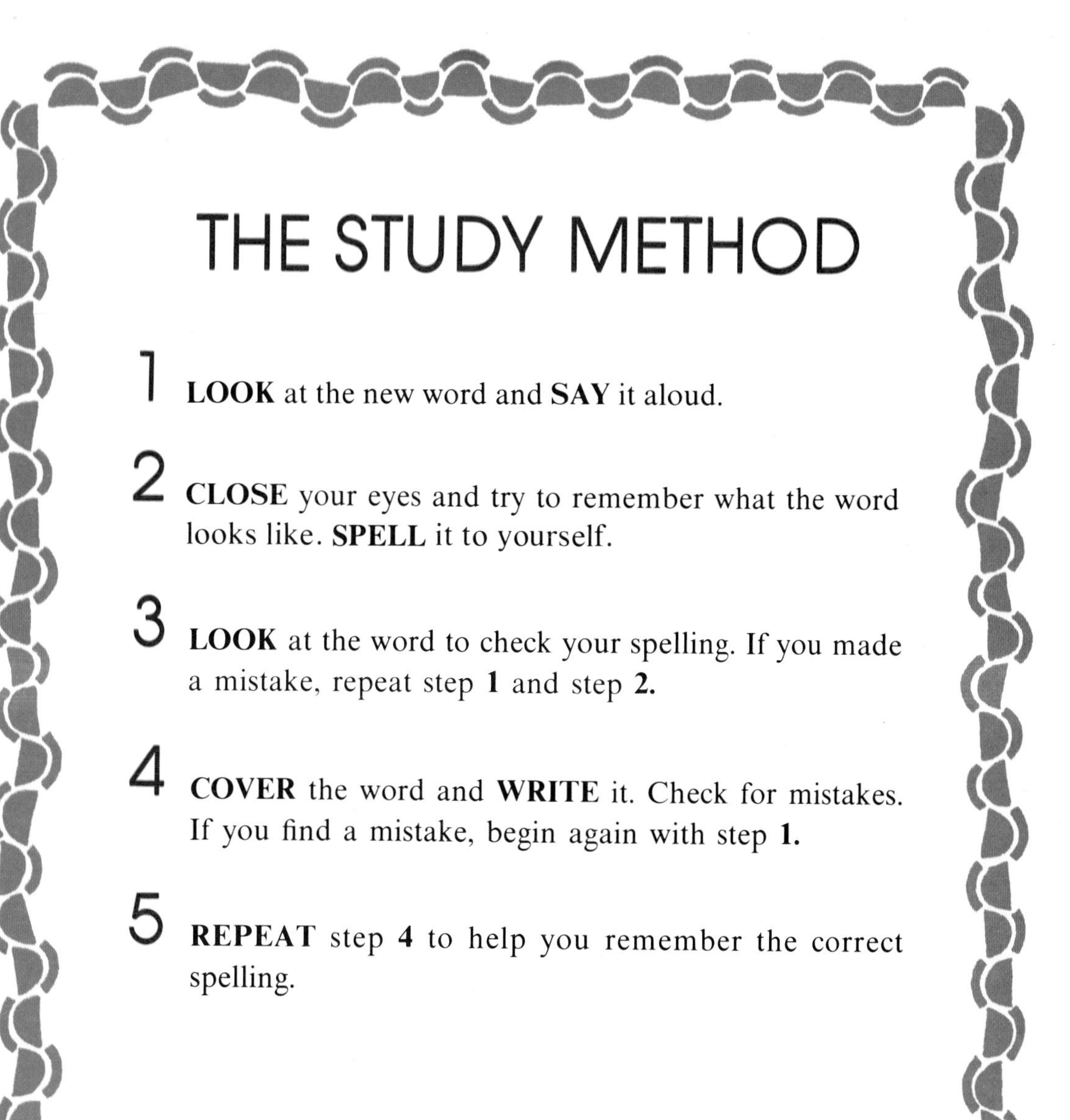

THE STUDY METHOD

1 **LOOK** at the new word and **SAY** it aloud.

2 **CLOSE** your eyes and try to remember what the word looks like. **SPELL** it to yourself.

3 **LOOK** at the word to check your spelling. If you made a mistake, repeat step **1** and step **2.**

4 **COVER** the word and **WRITE** it. Check for mistakes. If you find a mistake, begin again with step **1.**

5 **REPEAT** step **4** to help you remember the correct spelling.

Homophone hunt

Say the words
pear and *pair*.
How do these words sound
when you say them?

In what two ways
are they different?

Words that sound alike
but have different
spellings and meanings
are called *homophones*.
Write a homophone
for each of the words
in the list below.

1 hear
2 through
3 sun
4 merry
5 right
6 hole

1 Word shrinkers

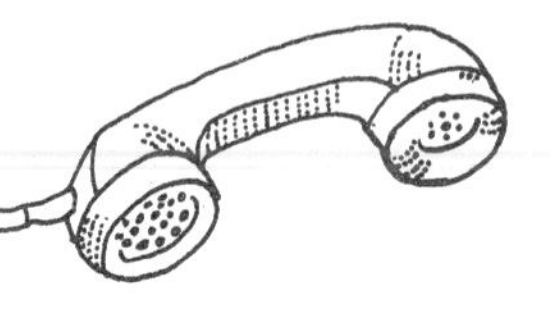

A Read the following sentences.
Della does not know Rita's phone number.
Della doesn't know Rita's phone number.

1 What is the difference
between the sentences?

2 What letter was left out of *not*
when it was connected to *does*
in the second sentence above?

3 What punctuation mark shows
that a letter has been left out?

4 What are words
like *doesn't* called?

A *contraction* is formed when
two words are joined
and one or more letters
are left out of the spelling.
An *apostrophe* (') is used to show
where any letters were left out.

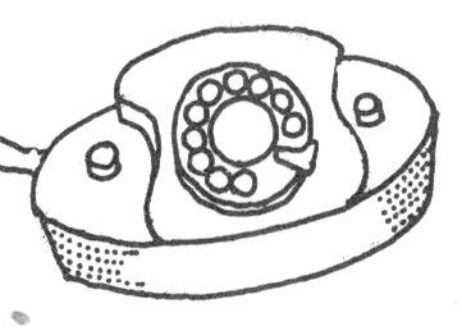

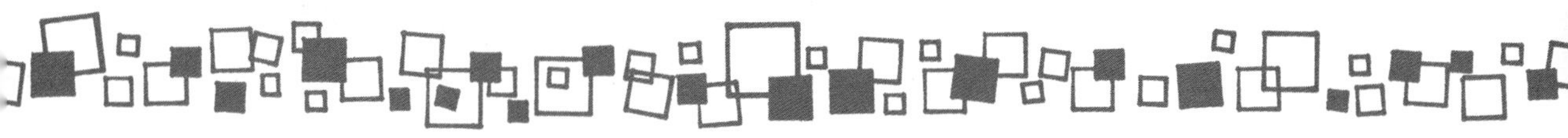

Sound code

A When we are writing about sounds in this book, we use a sound code. We show sound codes inside slanted lines like these / /. All of the sound codes used in this book are shown in the pronunciation key on page 122.

1 Listen to the vowel sound in *bat*. The sound code for the vowel sound in *bat* is /a/. Think of four words that have the same vowel sound as *bat*. Write those words. Then circle the vowel letter in each word that stands for /a/, as in *bat*.

2 Listen to the vowel sound in *pin*. The sound code for the vowel sound in *pin* is /i/. Think of four words that have the same vowel sound as *pin*. Write those words. Then circle the vowel letter in each word that stands for /i/, as in *pin*.

3 Listen to the beginning sound in *bear*. The sound code for the first sound you hear in *bear* is /b/. Think of four words that have the same consonant sound as the *b* in *bear*. Write those words. Circle the letter in each word that stands for /b/, as in *bear*.

B Become a word shrinker. Write the contraction for each of these words.

1 are not

2 has not

3 would not

4 do not

B

Say the words *whole* and *wrote*.
Listen to the beginning sound in each word.
Write the sound code for the sound you hear
at the beginning of each of the words.
Use the pronunciation key on page 122
if you need help.

whole wrote

1 How is /h/ most often spelled in words?

2 How is /h/ spelled in the word *whole?*

3 How is /r/ most often spelled in words?

4 How is /r/ spelled in the word *wrote?*

C

Think of two words
that begin with /h/
spelled *wh*.
Write those words.
Then think of two words
that begin with /r/
spelled *wr*.
Write those words.

The word search

Horsefeathers!

That's a funny word.
Hum is a quiet word.
What words do you think
are funny words
or quiet words?

Read the list of words
on the next page.
Think of some words
to add to each group.
You can look
in newspapers
or books for words.
Or you could make up
some new words!

1 Happy words
jolly, yippee, sunny

2 Sad words
glum, cry, aw

3 Funny words
humdinger, ha, kumquat

4 Quiet words
mouse, cloud, still

5 Noisy words
howl, bang, factory

6 Angry words
yell, grumpy, No!

7 Size words
huge, mile, long

8 Fast words
whiz, zipping, jet

9 Made-up words
poggy-wog, zoop, wrel

10 Science words
discover, germ, solar

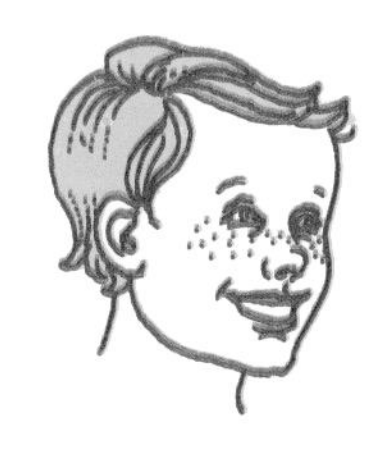

Word wonder

A single word
can give you
an idea for writing.

happiness

Happiness is going to the circus.

What do you think of when you read
each of the words at the right?
Write a sentence for each word.

happiness	freedom
laughter	friendship
love	life

/ī/ as in Kite

2

A Say the following words.
Listen to the vowel sound you hear
in each one of them.

bike die spider buy dry

Did you hear /ī/ in all of the above words?

Make a chart like the one below to show
the different spellings of /ī/. On your chart,
write *bike, die, spider, buy,* and *dry*
in separate columns. Circle the letter or letters
that spell /ī/. Then write these letters in the
first box above each of the words. The first two
have been done for you as examples.

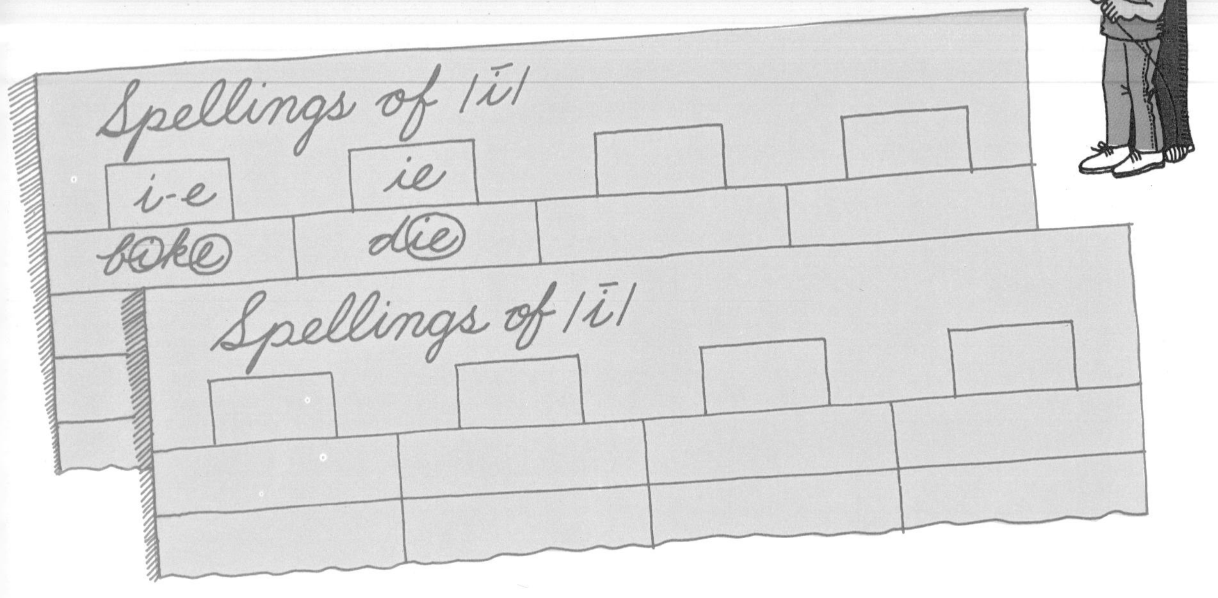

Often the *i*-consonant-*e* pattern
can spell /ī/, as *ite* in *kite*.
This spelling pattern is shown as *i-e*.

B Say the following words. Listen for /ī/.

alike quite wide

How is /ī/ spelled in each word? Write each of the words in the
correct column of your chart. Circle the letters that spell /ī/.

C Now say the words *sigh* and *bright*.
Notice how /ī/ is spelled in these two words.
Write *sigh* and *bright* in a new column.

In *sigh* and *bright*, /ī/ is spelled with three letters. Circle the three letters that spell /ī/ in the words you wrote on your chart. Write the letters in the box above the words.

D How many spellings of /ī/ does your chart show now?
Look for other words with /ī/. Put each word you find in the column that shows the same spelling of /ī/. If you find different spellings of /ī/, begin new columns on your chart.

Singular noun + apostrophe + s = possessive noun

A Read the following sentences.
Mike has a spider. The spider is a good spinner.
Mike's spider is a good spinner.

What has been added to the word *Mike* in the third sentence to show that the spider belongs to Mike?

We add an apostrophe and *s* ('s) to singular nouns to show possession or ownership.
The thing owned comes next, as in the example Mike'*s spider*.

Read the following pairs of sentences.
Then join each pair of sentences into one sentence using a possessive noun.

1 Maria has a bike. The bike is often beside this sign.

2 Rusty has a baseball. The baseball is quite old.

3 Ellen has a cabin. The cabin is in the country.

Dictionary pronunciation codes

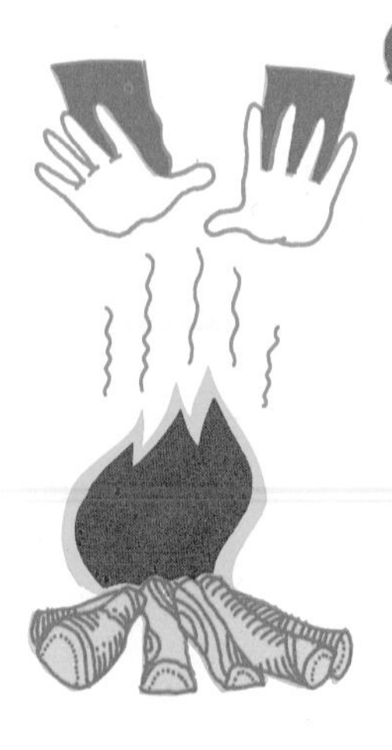

A

How would you find out how to say a new word? If the word *heat* were a new word to you, you might not be sure whether it should be pronounced with /e/, as in *bread*, or /ē/, as in *treat*. By looking in a dictionary you can find the correct pronunciation.

Find *heat* in your Spelling Dictionary. Study the pronunciation code that you see beside the word *heat*. The pronunciation code is the part between the slanted lines. It looks like this.

/hēt/

In writing, each vowel letter and some consonant letters can spell more than one sound. So, dictionaries use sound codes to show how the letters in a word are pronounced. The sound codes inside the slanted lines show how the word is pronounced.

Sound codes are sometimes different in different dictionaries. Each dictionary has a pronunciation key. If you need help in understanding a certain sound code used in a dictionary, you should check the key words for that sound. The pronunciation key for your Spelling Dictionary is on page 122.

B

Listed at the right are pronunciation codes for several words. Say each one. Then write the spelling for each word. Remember to use the pronunciation key on page 122 if you are not sure how a certain sound code should be pronounced. Then, after you have written each of the words, check your spellings in your Spelling Dictionary. The first one has been done for you.

1 /ˈmau̇nt-n/ *mountain*

2 /ant/ **3** /wōk/ **4** /kās/

5 /bläk/ **6** /nīf/ **7** /rek/

8 /ˈrath-ər/ **9** /wȯl/ **10** /spät/

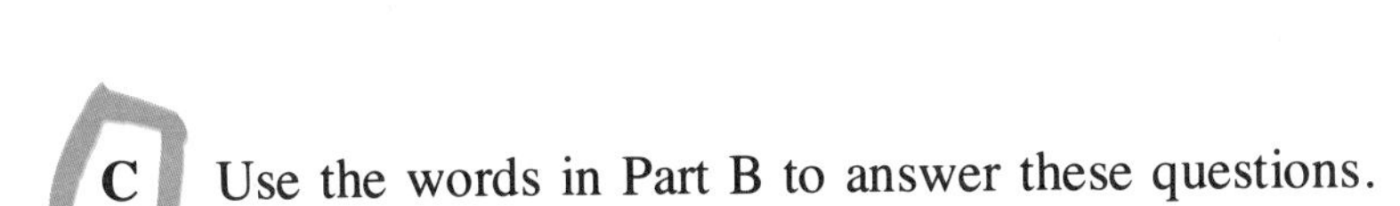

C Use the words in Part B to answer these questions.

1 What letter spells /k/ in /kās/?
2 What letter spells /k/ in /wōk/?
3 What letters spell /k/ in /bläk/ and /rek/?
4 What letters spell /n/ in /nīf/?
5 What letters spell /r/ in /rek/?
6 What letter spells /s/ in /spät/?

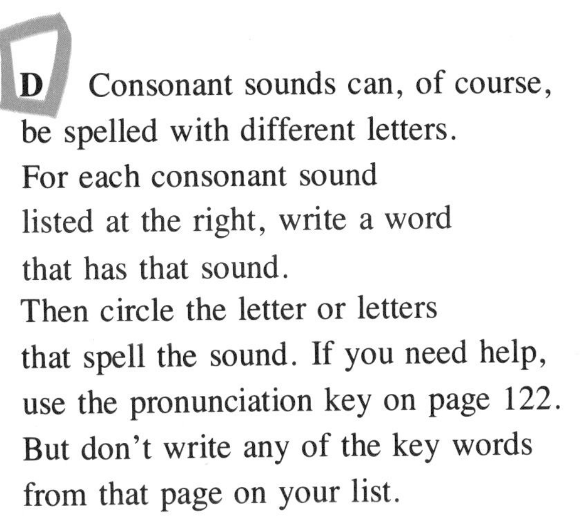

D Consonant sounds can, of course, be spelled with different letters. For each consonant sound listed at the right, write a word that has that sound. Then circle the letter or letters that spell the sound. If you need help, use the pronunciation key on page 122. But don't write any of the key words from that page on your list.

/b/	/k/	/t/
/ch/	/l/	/th/
/d/	/m/	/th/
/f/	/n/	/v/
/g/	/ng/	/w/
/h/	/p/	/y/
/hw/	/r/	/z/
/j/	/s/	/zh/
	/sh/	

Giving directions

It is important that directions be very clear and correct.

A set of directions should have these steps:

1 The first sentence or the title should tell what the directions are about.
2 Then any special materials needed should be listed.
3 The steps in the directions should be given in correct order.

Write directions for doing or making something. Be sure to put in all of the necessary steps and materials in your directions.

/ȯi/ as in Joy

3

Say the words below.
Listen to the vowel sound they all have.

toy	oyster	joy
oil	foil	soil

The vowel sound that you hear in all of these words is /ȯi/.

What are two spellings of /ȯi/?

Make two lists for spellings of /ȯi/.
Write each of the six words that are listed above
in the correct column, "/ȯi/ spelled *oy*" or "/ȯi/ spelled *oi*."

/ȯi/ spelled **oy**	/ȯi/ spelled **oi**

Look for other words
that have /ȯi/ in them.
Add these words
to the correct column,
"/ȯi/ spelled *oy*"
or "/ȯi/ spelled *oi*."
You will want
to add these lists
to your spelling folder,
which contains
your chart for spellings
of /ī/.

C

Use the words you have written that have /ȯi/
in them to answer the following questions.

1 How is /ȯi/ spelled
at the end of a word?

2 How is /ȯi/ spelled
in the middle of a word?

3 How is /ȯi/ spelled
at the beginning
of a word?

Syllables

Say the following words.

alike alive

baseball spider cabin

How many vowel sounds do you hear in each of the above words?

There is a *syllable*, or word division, for each pronounced vowel in a word. How many syllables do the above words have?

Say the following words.
Write the number of syllables each word has.

1 quite **2** often **3** decide

4 September **5** rubber **6** sigh

7 potato **8** telephone

Accented syllables

When a word has more than one syllable, part of the word is pronounced more loudly. The syllable pronounced more loudly has an accent mark in its pronunciation code.

Look at the following examples of word division. Each shows the accented syllable. Say the words.

'cab in de 'cide

The first syllable of the word *cabin* is pronounced more loudly, so the accent mark is placed by the first syllable. The second syllable of the word *decide* is pronounced more loudly, so the accent mark is placed by the second syllable.

Say the following words.
Copy each word as it appears below. Put an accent mark in front of the syllable that is pronounced more loudly. Then to check your work, look at the pronunciation code for each word in your Spelling Dictionary.

1 cer tain **3** tick et **5** a like
2 rub ber **4** a wake **6** sur prise

What's missing? abcdefghijklmnopqrstuvwxyzab

A Below are pronunciation codes for five words. Say each word and write its correct spelling. If you are not sure how a sound code is pronounced, use the pronunciation key on page 122.
Use your Spelling Dictionary to check the spellings of the words.

1 /ˈhwis-əl/ **3** /ˈsȯf-ən/ **5** /ˈfas-n/
2 /ˈkas-əl/ **4** /ˈlis-n/

B

1 In each of the words in part A which syllable is accented? Which one is not accented?

2 Which letter is not pronounced in each of the first three words?

3 Which letters are not pronounced in each of the last two words?

4 Circle letters that aren't pronounced in each of the words you wrote.

5 Which of the words have a syllable without a vowel sound?

Past forms

A Read the following sentences.
The verb is underlined in each sentence.

> Cindy <u>talks</u> about her vacation all the time.
>
> Cindy <u>talked</u> about her vacation all the time.

1 Which verb, *talks* or *talked*, shows that the action is in the past?

2 What was added to the verb *talk* to make the past form?

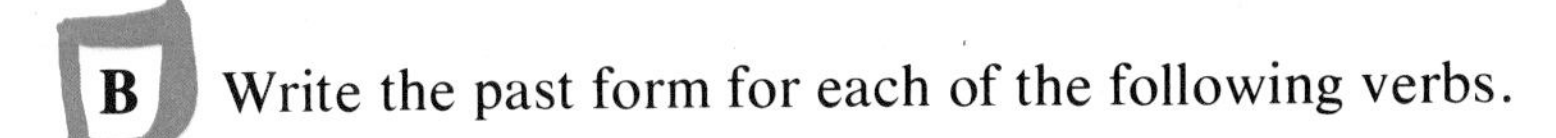

B Write the past form for each of the following verbs.

1 finish **6** act

2 wreck **7** attack

3 point **8** bowl

4 join **9** follow

5 enjoy **10** reach

What letters did you add to each of the verbs above to make the past form?

Any verb whose past form is made by adding **-ed** is called a *regular verb*.

C Below is another list of verbs. Write the past form for each one.

1 wake **5** write **8** buy

2 ride **6** build **9** drive

3 pay **7** feel **10** spend

4 fly

Check the past tense forms in your Spelling Dictionary to be certain you spelled them correctly.

Do these verbs follow the regular pattern by adding **-ed** to make the past form?

Since these verbs don't follow the regular pattern to make the past form, they are called *irregular verbs*. Can you think of any other irregular verbs?

Idea + Imagination = Story

Read each group of words below. Choose one group to write a story about, or make up your own group of words to write about.

- softball, pitcher, strike two, roar of laughter
- moon, earth, mysterious planet, astronauts, lost
- time machine, past, future, broken, trapped

Contractions — which word is shortened? 4

A People almost always use contractions in speaking. And very often people will use contractions in writing. Read the following sentence.

I'm ready to go, but Stephen isn't.

What contractions are used in the sentence above? Here is how these two contractions are formed.

I + am = I~~a~~m = I'm
is + not = isn~~o~~t = isn't

Given in the following activity are words from which contractions can be formed. Write the words as they appear below, first as separate words and then joined. Cross out the letters in the joined words that should be left out when the contraction is formed. Then, write the correct form for each contraction. The first one has been done for you.

1 I + will	I~~wi~~ll *I'll*		**6** can + not	cannot
2 they + have	theyhave		**7** we + are	weare
3 he + is	heis		**8** I + have	Ihave
4 she + is	sheis		**9** you + have	youhave
5 there + is	thereis		**10** of + the + clock	oftheclock

When you combine words to form a contraction, from which word are the letters usually left out?

Which contraction you wrote does not follow that pattern?

B Do the crossword puzzle on page 15 by writing contractions for the words that are given. There is a separate box for the apostrophe used in each contraction.

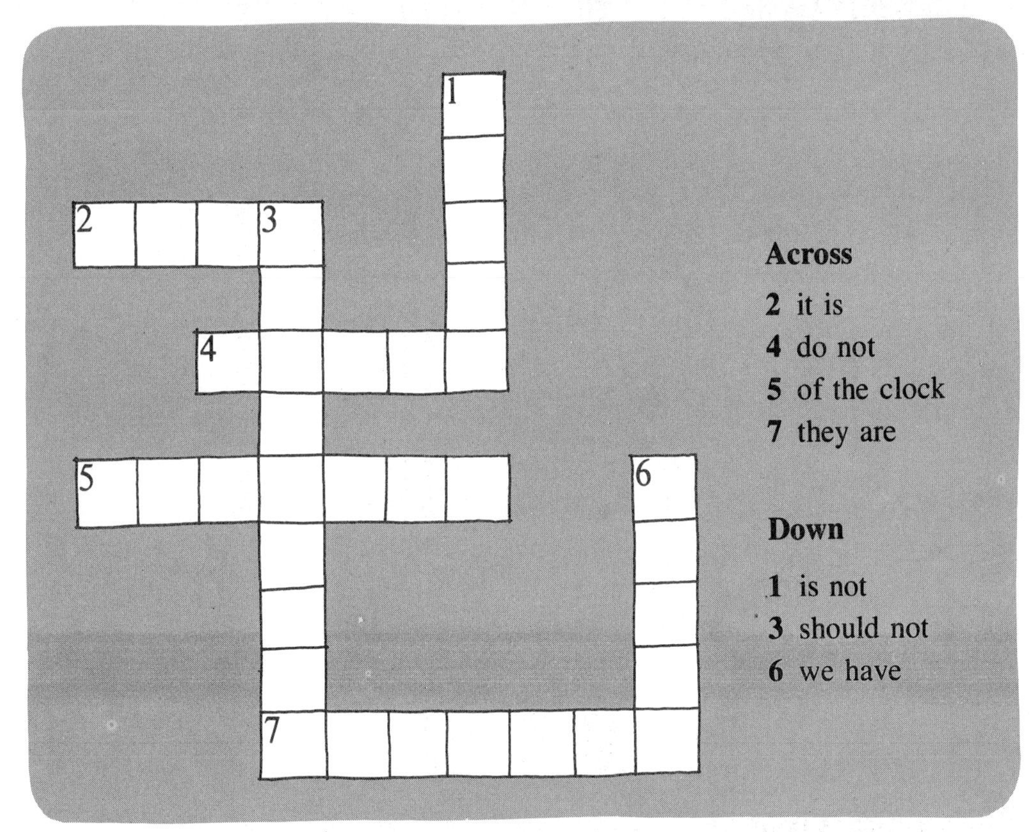

/z/ as in the *Zooming Bees Buzzed* by

A The same sound may be spelled with different letters in different words. Say the following words.

zoo his buzz size raise surprise

1 What sound do you hear in all of the above words?

2 What letter spells /z/ in *zoo?*

3 What letter spells /z/ in *his?*

4 What two letters spell /z/ in *buzz?*

5 What letter spells /z/ in *size?*

6 What letter spells /z/ in *raise?*

7 What letter spells / z/ in *surprise?*

B Listed below are pronunciation codes for several words. Say each word. Then write the spelling for each word. Use the pronunciation key on page 122 if you are not sure how a sound code should be pronounced. After you have written all of the words, check your spellings in the Spelling Dictionary.

1 /hēz/

2 /sər-ˈprīz/

3 /ˈhaz-nt/

4 /frēz/

5 /sīz/

6 /zü/

Sound codes

A dictionary usually has a complete pronunciation key in the front of the book. A dictionary will also usually have a short pronunciation key at the bottom of every page or every other page.

The following list is part of a dictionary pronunciation key. It's a list of vowel sound codes with a key word to show how the sound code is pronounced.

Look at each sound code. Say the key word that has the sound that code stands for. Then write another word that has the same vowel sound. Circle the letter or letters in the word you wrote that spell that sound.

Sound codes	Key words	Sound codes	Key words
1 /a/	bat	8 /ī/	kite
2 /ā/	ape	9 /ō/	boat
3 /ä/	top	10 /ȯ/	saw
4 /au̇/	owl	11 /ȯi/	oil
5 /e/	elf	12 /ü/	moon
6 /ē/	eel	13 /u̇/	foot
7 /i/	pin	14 /ə/	cup

From pronunciation to spelling

Listed below are pronunciation codes for sixteen words.
Use the Spelling Dictionary pronunciation key on page 122
to help you pronounce each of the words.
Then write the correct spelling of each word.

1 /lēd/
2 /'kab-ən/
3 /pȯint/
4 /'mau̇nt-n/
5 /hȯrn/
6 /drōv/
7 /grü/
8 /twelv/
9 /brāv/
10 /ə-'hwīl/
11 /mēl/
12 /'kich-ən/
13 /'ȯr-inj/
14 /'shu̇d-nt/
15 /äk-'tō-bər/
16 /hwēl/

Capture a color

What Is Gold?

Gold is a ripe pear, fat and juicy.
Gold is a goldfish swimming in a pool.
Gold is bright yellow hair
shining in the sunlight.
Gold is bags and bags of money.
Gold is a lonely daisy in a field.

Purple Is

Purple is a bunch of grapes.
Purple is a mountain range.
Purple is a royal color
worn by kings and queens.
Purple is a flower.
Purple is the sky at night.

What objects do you think of when you think of a certain color?
Capture your favorite color on paper. Write about it.
As you write your thoughts, begin each new idea
on a new line. Give your ''color writing'' a title.

/ē/ as in See the Sleepy Seal 5

A Say the following words. Listen to the vowel sound that is the same in all of them.

seal wheel movie tiny

Did you hear /ē/ in all of the above words?

Make a chart like the one below to show the different spellings of /ē/.
On your chart, write *seal, wheel, movie,* and *tiny* in separate columns.
Circle the letter or letters that spell /ē/.
Then write these letters in the box above each word.
The first one has been done for you as an example.

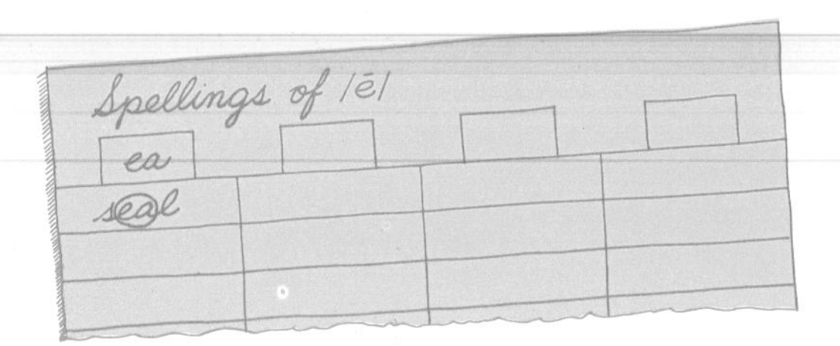

B Say the following words. Listen for /ē/.

east chief fifty coffee

How is /ē/ spelled in each word?
Write each of the words
in the correct column of your chart.
Circle the letters that spell /ē/.

C Now say the following words.

honey he's cheese

How is /ē/ spelled in each of the words above?
Write each word in a separate column.
Circle the letter or letters that spell /ē/.
Then write these letters
in the box above each of the words.

D How many spellings of /ē/ does your chart show now?
Look for other words with /ē/. Put each word you find in the column that shows the same spelling of /ē/. If you find different spellings of /ē/, begin new columns on your chart.

Put your chart
for the spellings of /ē/
in your folder
for spellings of sounds.

/ər/ as in a Certain Surprise

A Say the following words.
Listen to the sound they all have.

term swirl firm
curl burn serve

1 Is the vowel letter the same in all of the words above?

2 Is the consonant letter that comes
after the first vowel letter
the same in all of the words above?

3 What is the consonant letter
that follows the vowel letter in each word above?

4 Do *er, ir,* and *ur* spell
the same sound in all of the words listed above?

B Say these words.

worm learn collar
work heard sugar
word earn dollar

1 Do you hear /ər/
in each of these words?

2 What letters
are used to spell that sound
in the words listed above?

C What vowel letters
may combine with *r* to spell /ər/?

Look at the following list of words.
Make another word from each word
in the list by adding *r*
after the vowel letter. Then say each
pair of words and listen
for the change in the vowel sound.

1 gem **2** hut **3** bun

4 head **5** bid

6 cub **7** fist **8** lean

Using a key to unlock words

Use the pronunciation key
on page 122 to help you
pronounce each word below.
Then write the correct spelling
for each word.

1 /sēl/

2 /sər-ˈprīz/

3 /hwēl/

4 /ˈtī-nē/

5 /ˈpər-pəl/

6 /fər/

7 /ˈkȯf-ē/

8 /ˈsər-kəl/

9 /wərm/

10 /ˈmü-vē/

11 /sep-ˈtem-bər/

12 /ˈrath-ər/

13 /ˈfif-tē/

14 /ˈrəb-ər/

15 /mēl/

16 /ˈshu̇g-ər/

17 /äk-ˈtō-bər/

18 /ˈməth-ərz/

Check your spelling of each word in your Spelling Dictionary.

Using a dictionary for spelling

A When you want to use a new word in writing, you can be certain of its spelling by checking it in a dictionary. To use a dictionary for spelling, you need to have some idea of the possible spellings of the word you want to write.

In Unit 1 you learned two possible spellings of /h/ and of /r/ at the beginning of a word. What are the two possible spellings of /h/ when it is at the beginning of a word?

Pronounce the following word. /hōl/

There are two words that are pronounced /hōl/. Do you know how to spell the two words? To find both words, look in your Spelling Dictionary under the two possible
spellings of /h/. Write both words.

B Write the correct spelling of /hōl/ for each sentence below.

1 Who ate the ____ piece of cheese?

2 The spider went through the ____ in the screen.

3 The seal made a big ____ in the barrel.

4 Andy wiggled like a worm through the ____ meal.

5 A ____ group of us dug that huge ____ in the ground to bury our treasure.

C Pronounce the following words. Find the correct spellings in your Spelling Dictionary and write them.

1 /hüz/ **3** /ˈhap-ən/

2 /hēt/ **4** /helth/

D What are the two possible spellings of /r/ when it is at the beginning of a word?

Pronounce each of the following words. Find the correct spellings in your Spelling Dictionary and write them.

1 /rōt/ **2** /rek/ **3** /rīs/ **4** /rēch/

Picture a pet

Imagine that you have just found a very unusual pet. It might be a purple worm, a furry spider, a tiny seal, an orange wolf, or just anything you can imagine. Now suppose you took your unusual pet to school or for a walk one day. Write a story about your adventures together. In your story you might tell about these things.

where you met your unusual pet

its name

its size, color, and shape

what your friends or people you met thought of your pet

how you plan to take care of it

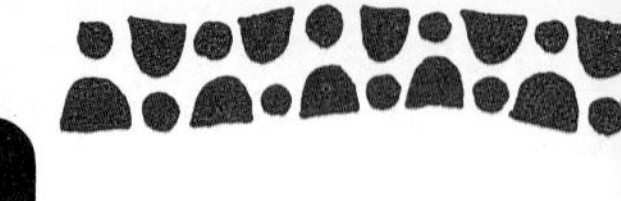

/ō/ as in Oh! a Ghost! 6

A Say the following words.
Listen to the vowel sound
that is the same in all of them.

ghost follow goat alone

Did you hear /ō/
in all of the above words?

Make a chart like the one below
to show the different spellings of /ō/.
On your chart, write *ghost, follow, goat,* and *alone*
in separate columns. Circle the letter or letters that spell /ō/.
Then write these letters in the box above each word.
The first one has been done for you as an example.

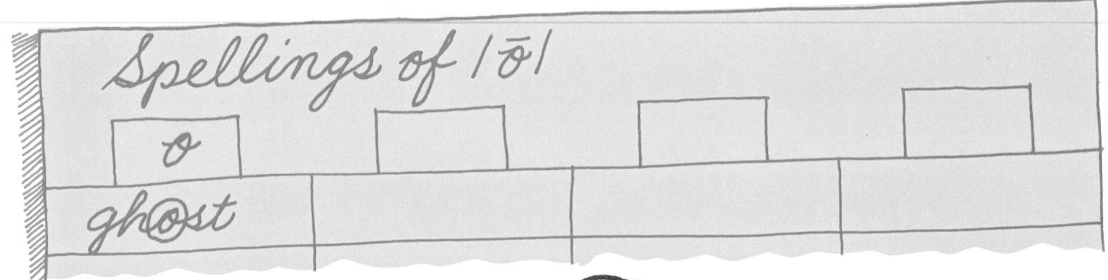

B Say the following words.
Listen for /ō/.

ocean drove bowl coal

How is /ō/ spelled in each word?
Write each of the words
in the correct column
of your chart. Circle
the letters that spell /ō/.

C Now say the word *though*.
What is the last sound you hear?
Write *though* in a separate column
on your chart. In *though*,
/ō/ is spelled with four letters.
Circle these letters in the word
you wrote on the chart.
Write the letters in the box
above the word.

D How many spellings of /ō/ does your chart show now?
Look for other words with /ō/. Put each word you find in the column
that shows the same spelling of /ō/. If you find different spellings
of /ō/, begin new columns on your chart.

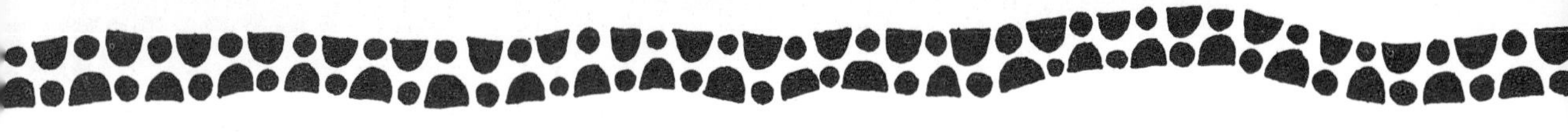

Which Witch?

A Say the words *which* and *witch*. Do they sound alike to you?
To some people these words sound alike. They both begin with /w/.
To other people, *witch* begins with /w/, but *which* begins with /hw/.

Do *which* and *witch* have the same meaning?
Although they may sound alike to some people, these words have different meanings and different spellings.

Write the correct word, *which* or *witch*, for each sentence below.

1 The ____ was getting ready for Halloween night.
2 But she couldn't decide ____ broom to ride.
3 "Well, ____ color do you like better, black or orange?" asked another ____.
4 ____ one do you think the ____ will want to ride on Halloween night?

B Now say *which* and *witch* again.
Do you hear /ch/ in both words?

How is /ch/ spelled in *which?*

How is /ch/ spelled in *witch*?

To the right are pronunciation codes for several words.
Write the correct spelling for each word.
Then, in each word you wrote, circle the letters that spell /ch/.

1 /ˈkich-ən/
2 /inch/
3 /bēch/
4 /ˈkach-ər/
5 /chēz/
6 /ranch/
7 /mach/
8 /pach/

Is /ch/ ever spelled *tch* at the beginning of a word?
You can check your Spelling Dictionary to answer this question.

A tricky tale

In Unit 1 you learned that words that sound alike but have different spellings and different meanings are called homophones. Read this tale carefully. There are eighteen wrong homophones in it. Rewrite the tale using the correct words. Underline each word you changed.

Once their was a very plane which. She had bright orange hair that she brushed with a big read brush. After the son went down on Halloween knight, she wood fly threw the sky two sea the scarecrows in the fields. Each Halloween she chose a new scarecrow king four the year.

The scarecrows loved her bright orange hair and her friendly weighs. And they could hardly weight each year for Halloween to see witch won of them she wood choose too bee the scarecrow king for the year.

Write Right!

Listed below are several pairs of homophones. Beside each pair of homophones are two sentences. Write the correct homophone for each sentence.

1 plain plane
- **a** When we drove across the _____ , we saw antelope.
- **b** Rich and Greg flew the _____ to Boston yesterday.

2 bear bare
- **a** Joel thought the room looked _____ with the chair gone.
- **b** I saw a grizzly _____ when I was in Alaska.

3 through threw
- **a** Quickly, Kim _____ the ball to the first baseman.
- **b** After the game, we had to struggle _____ the crowd.

4 theirs there's
- **a** Well, who can take _____ to them today?
- **b** I'll bet _____ nobody at the park since it's raining.

Halloween happenings

Hundreds of years ago in England, Halloween was
a night of fear. People believed that ghosts, witches,
and other evil spirits came out on Halloween night.
So, everyone lit huge bonfires to keep them away.
People also cut holes in turnips
and placed candles inside them to keep the evil spirits from harming them.

But now Halloween, the night of October 31, is a night of fun and adventure.
It's the night you can light jack-o-lanterns and have parties.
It's the night you can dress up in scary costumes,
especially ghost and witch costumes, and go trick-or-treating.

Pretend it is Halloween. You've been trick-or-treating
and are on your way home now. Write a tale about a spooky Halloween happening.
Draw a picture about your tale.

Crossword puzzle

Do this crossword puzzle on a piece of paper by supplying
the correct Halloween words.

Across
2 a fruit we bob for (plural)
4 trick-or- ____
6 October 31
8 usual Halloween treats
9 a large, outdoor fire

Down
1 a pumpkin cut out
to look like a face
3 bones fitted together
5 the spirit of one
who is dead
appearing to the living
7 a woman believed to have
magic powers

/ə/ as in Such a Purple Princess 7

A Say each word below.
Listen to the sound
the underlined vowel letter spells.

awake women family

apron upon

Each underlined vowel
in the words above
spells the same sound.
The sound is called *schwa*
and the sound code for schwa is /ə/.

Look again at the vowel letters
used to spell /ə/.
What vowel letters can spell /ə/?

Make a chart like the one below to show the different spellings of /ə/.
On your chart, write the following words in separate columns.

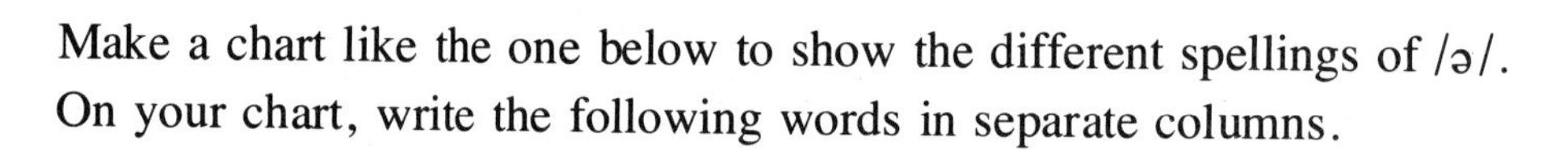

awake women family apron upon

Circle the letter that spells /ə/ in each word you wrote. Then write the letter
in the box above each word. The first one has been done for you.

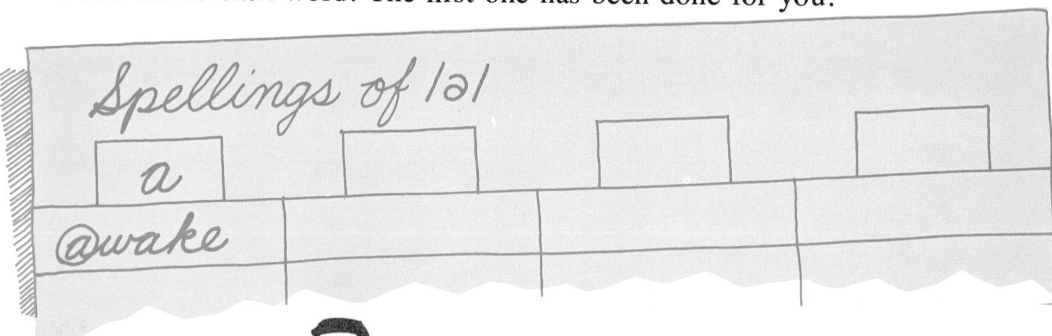

B Say the word *America*.
Write *America* in the two correct columns on your chart.
Circle the three vowels that spell /ə/.
Check your Spelling Dictionary to see if you are right.

C Say the following words.

breakfast
princess
cabin
wagon
such

Do you hear /ə/
in each word above?
Write each word
in the correct column on your chart.
Circle the letter
that spells /ə/
in each word you wrote.

D Now say the words below.

sugar doctor
answer surprise
dirty earth

Do you hear /ər/ in each word?
Make a new chart for /ər/.
Write each of the above words
in a separate column.
Circle the letters
in each word that spell /ər/.
Then write those letters
in the box above each word.

What vowel letters can combine
with *r* to spell /ər/?

E How many columns
for spellings of /ə/
does your first chart have?

How many columns
for spellings of /ər/
does your second chart have?

Look for other words with /ə/.
Put each word you find
in the column that shows
the same spelling of /ə/.
If you find different spellings of /ə/,
begin new columns on your chart.

Look for other words with /ər/, too.
Put each word you find
in the column that shows
the same spelling of /ər/.

Build new words

A Our written language slowly changes. When two or more words are often used together, people begin writing them as one word. A *compound word* is two or more words that are written together.

Read the two lists of words below. Make compound words by choosing words from the second column to combine with words in the first column.

1 play	night
2 news	stairs
3 up	place
4 police	ground
5 mid	man
6 bed	paper
7 fire	room
8 sail	boat

B Write a compound word for each definition given below. The first one has been done for you.

1 a bowl used to keep fish in *fishbowl*

2 a brush used to clean teeth

3 a cloth that covers a table

4 a hook for catching fish

5 a yard for storing junk

6 the time a meal is served

7 a boat that is rowed

8 a track on which races are run

9 the light of day

10 the beat of a heart

11 corn that pops when heated

12 a string used for tying shoes

Word snapshots

To describe an object, a happening, or a scene, writers can use words that tell how it looks, feels, sounds, tastes, or smells. In other words, the writer uses words that appeal to our senses.

Write words that appeal to the senses for the things that are given below. The first few have been done for you.

1 fudge brownies *warm, sweet chocolate*

2 a police siren *shrill*

3 lemon *sunshine yellow*

4 hog's hair

5 thunder

6 cotton candy

7 a thorn

8 a bunch of roses

9 puppy fur

10 skyscrapers

Snap the seasons

Autumn is a silent rain
of yellow, gold, and orange.

Autumn is a loud crunch
of leaves beneath my feet.

Candy apples, yummy and gooey,
are a must for autumn time.

And autumn always brings football fun
in the stiff, cool autumn breeze.

Autumn, winter, spring, and summer are the names of the four seasons of the year. Choose one of the seasons. Write a poem about what that season means to you. In your writing, use words that appeal to the senses.

Base + suffix = new word 8

A A *suffix* is an addition put at the end of a base word. It changes a word's meaning. Look up the suffixes **-ful** and **-less** in a dictionary. The hyphen (-) before each suffix shows that it is not a complete word. A suffix must be added to the end of a base word.

The suffix **-ful** means "full of" or "enough to fill." The suffix **-less** means "without" or "that does not." Read the following examples.

Angie was careful not to spill the beans.

Angie was full of care so she would not spill the beans.

Batman is tireless and fearless.

Batman does not tire and is without fear.

Listed below are six words. Add **-less** or **-ful** to each of the words to make a new word. Write a sentence for each new word you made.

1 care **2** thank **3** help **4** pain **5** watch **6** use

B For each of the definitions given below, write a base word with the suffix **-less** or **-ful** added. Then write sentences using the new words you wrote.

1 without stars
2 enough to fill a spoon
3 without a point
4 enough to fill a sack
5 enough to fill a pipe
6 enough to fill a glass
7 without sight
8 that does not have sugar

Adding -er and -est to base words

A Read the following sentences.

A kitten is small.
A spider is smaller than a kitten.
An ant is smallest of the three.

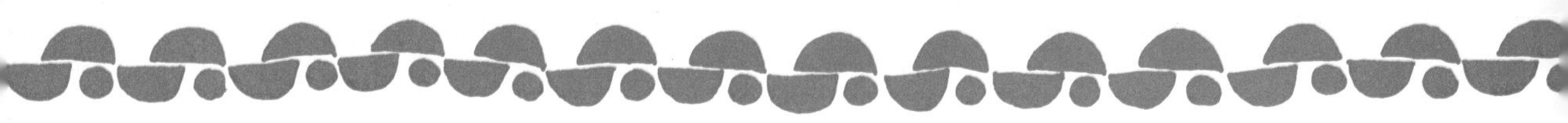

The underlined words in the sentences you just read are *adjectives*.

The **-er** form of an adjective is used when two persons or things are being compared. The **-est** form of an adjective is used when more than two persons or things are being compared.

1 Which underlined word is a base word only?

2 Which underlined word is used to compare three things?

3 Which underlined word is used to compare two things?

B The following patterns apply when you want to add **-er** or **-est** to a base word.

When a word ends in one vowel and one consonant, double the consonant before adding **-er** or **-est.**
hot + er = hotter   hot + est = hottest

When a word ends with *e*, drop the *e* before adding **-er** or **-est.**
large + er = larger   large + est = largest

When a word ends with *y*, change the *y* to *i* before adding **-er** or **-est.**
pretty + er = prettier   pretty + est = prettiest

For all other words, just add **-er** or **-est.**
cheap + er = cheaper   cheap + est = cheapest

Make a chart like the one shown. Put each of the following words under the correct pattern word. Write the base word, the base word + **-er,** and the base word + **-est** for each word listed.

bright	silly
sunny	wide
brave	sad
short	thin
fat	plain
loose	dirty

hot	hotter	hottest	large	larger	largest
pretty	prettier	prettiest	cheap	cheaper	cheapest

Spin a word

Make a puzzle like the one shown. Read each numbered clue. Decide which of the words listed below the puzzle fits each clue. Write the word into the puzzle. Write the first letter of the word in the space with the same number as the clue. The other letters in the word go toward the center. The first answer has been done for you. When you have completed the puzzle, the inside circle will spell a mystery word. The outside circle will spell its meaning.

1 When you get a present, you ____ the giver.
2 flat or smooth
3 not at any time
4 a room just under the roof of a building
5 the part of a room you stand on
6 the one that is left (I had one mitt, John had the ____.)
7 a bird with a grayish back and a reddish breast
8 not soft or quiet; noisy
9 grew to be
10 a natural stream of water larger than a brook or creek
11 one more than seven
12 higher than; over
13 a person who watches, guards, or takes care of something
14 If it makes you laugh, it's ____.
15 a round fruit with red, yellow, or green skin

thank
small
robin
sea
they're

attic
eight
loud
floor
never

funny
animal
even
became
above

every
keeper
other
apple
river

16 little in size
17 contraction for *they are*
18 a body of salt water smaller than an ocean
19 all; each one
20 a living thing that is not a plant

Word power

A There's horsepower, jet power, and willpower.
But you've got word power! Read the following sentence.

The dog walked down the street.

Cut a piece of paper into squares, making each square about 2 inches by 2 inches. Write each word in the sentence above on one of the paper squares. Arrange the squares on your desk to make the sentence. Then read the following questions.

1 What kind of dog was it? Picture the dog in your mind. On separate squares of paper, write a few words that would describe the dog. Put a word or two into your sentence.

2 How was the dog walking? Think of two words that describe how the dog walked down the street. Put these words on separate squares. Which word do you like better? Put it in your sentence.

3 *Walked* is a weary word because it is used so often. What interesting word could you use in place of *walked?* Take the word *walked* out of the sentence. Write the new word on a square and put it in your sentence.

4 What kind of street did the dog walk down? On separate squares write a few words that describe the street. Put one or two of these new words into your sentence.

On another piece of paper, write your new sentence. Does it sound more interesting to you?

B Use word power to improve these plain sentences. Make word squares as you did in Part A, or just write the improved sentences on your paper.

1 The puppy looked at a bug.

2 A spider walked across its web.

3 A wolf went through the forest.

4 The seal swam in the water.

/ā/ as in Ape 9

A Say the following words.
Listen for the vowel sound
that is the same in all of them.

space paid clay they agent

Do you hear /ā/?
Make a chart like the one shown.
Write the words listed above
in separate columns on your chart.
Circle the letter or letters
that spell /ā/. Then write
the letters you circled
in the box above each column.
The first word has been done for you.

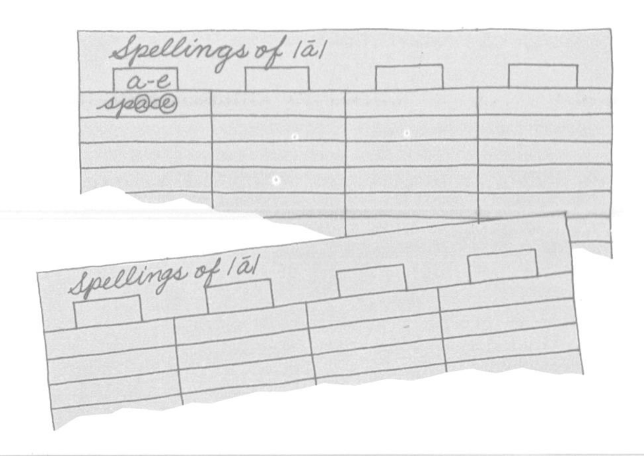

B Say the following words and listen for /ā/.

page apron day hey rain

How is /ā/ spelled in each word listed above?
Write each word in the correct column on your chart.
Circle the letters that spell /ā/.

C Now say the words *eight*
and *weight*. Which letters spell /ā/
in each word? Add these words
to your chart. Begin a new column
on your chart if necessary.
Circle the letters that spell /ā/
in each word you wrote.
Write the letters you circled
in the box above the words.

D Look for other words
with /ā/. Check several pages
of a reader or a library book.
Add words you find with /ā/
to your chart. You may need
to add new columns
to your chart.

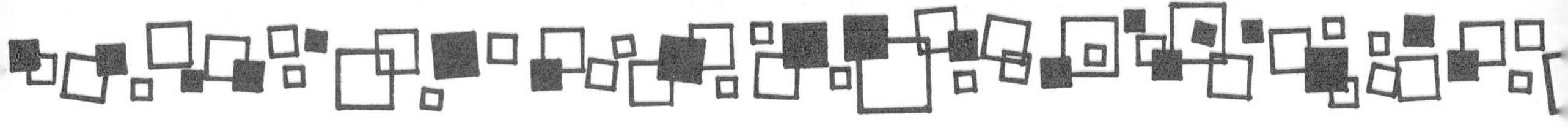

Alphabet agent

Long ago, the Greeks called the letter *a alpha* and the letter *b beta*. The Greek words *alpha* and *beta* became the English word *alphabet*.

How well do you know alphabetical order?
Become an alphabet agent.
Make four columns on a piece of paper.
Number the columns 1, 2, 3, and 4.
Then put the words from column 1 below in alphabetical order in column 1 on your paper.
Do columns 2, 3, and 4 the same way.

1	2	3	4
pound	wall	through	real
please	wagon	though	ready
page	wanted	thankful	reason
point	water	thin	read
plain	wait	threw	reach

Homophone hang-up

A What are homophones? If you don't remember, you may want to turn back to Unit 1 to find the answer to this question. Write your answer.

1 Say /thrü/. Write two ways this pronunciation code is spelled.

Circle the spelling of /ü/ in each of the homophones you wrote.
Then write a sentence for each homophone.

2 Now say /baər/. Write two ways this pronunciation code is spelled.

Circle the spelling of /aər/ in each of the homophones you wrote.
Then write a sentence for each homophone.

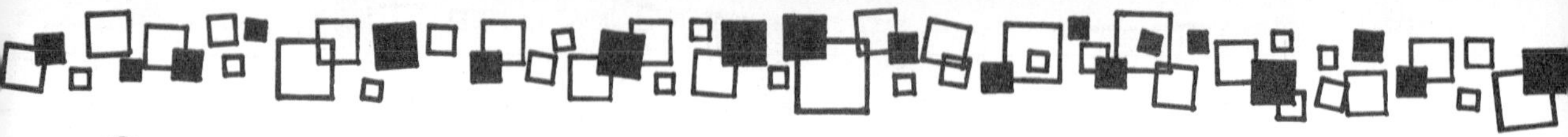

Extension. Say the words *rain*, *rein*, and *reign*. How are they alike?

How are they different?

Find the homophones *rain, rein*, and *reign* in a dictionary. Write each word, its pronunciation code, and one of its meanings. Then write a sentence for each word.

C

Make a homophone hang-up game. For this game you need some three-inch-by-five-inch cards.

Think of as many homophones as you can. Write each one on a separate card. On the back of the card, write the definition of the word you wrote. You may want to use a dictionary. On another set of cards, write only the word. Don't write the definition.

To play the game, spread the definition cards on a table. Put the definition side up so all of the definitions can be read. Place the set of cards that have only the words in a stack, face down. Take turns drawing a homophone card.

Draw only one card each turn. Try to match it with the correct definition card. Check the back of the definition card to see if you are right. If you match them correctly, you keep the pair of cards. If you are wrong, put the definition card back on the table and put the homophone card under the homophone stack.

You may set a time limit or you can play until all of the homophone cards are matched with their definitions. The player who has the most cards wins the game.

Code a riddle

Below are three riddles. Read each riddle and try to answer it.
Then look below at the answers. The answers are given
in pronunciation codes! Spell the correct words for the codes
and you'll have all the correct answers to the riddles.
You may want to use the pronunciation key on page 122 of your Spelling
Dictionary if you aren't sure what sound some of the codes stand for.

1 What do you call one cow
and two ducks?

2 When is a baseball player
like a spider?

3 There's a gray horse,
a black and white horse,
and a brown horse.
Which one of them
sings "Home on the Range"?

Answers to riddles

1 /milk/ /and/ /ˈkwak-ərz/

2 /hwen/ /hē/ /ˈkach-əz/ /ə/ /flī/

3 /nən/ /əv/ /them/
/ə/ /hȯrs/ /kant/ /sing/

Think of other riddles.
On a three-inch-by-five-inch
card, write the question.
(Remember to put
a question mark at the end
of the question.)
Turn the card over.
Use the pronunciation
codes to write
the answers
to the riddles.
You may want to use
the pronunciation
key on page 122
to write your codes
for the words.
Have other students
try to answer
your riddles.

Strange comparisons

How are a pencil and a grapefruit alike?
How does a pencil remind you
of a grapefruit?

A pencil and a grapefruit are alike because
both of them can be yellow,
both of them take up space,
I can chew on both of them, and
the best part is inside both of them.

Write an unusual or strange comparison.
Choose any two objects and compare them
in any way you can.
"A ____ reminds me of a ____ . . ."

/aů/ as in the Loud Clown Found a Brown Mouse

10

A Listen to /aů/, as in *owl*,
as you say each of the following words.

blouse crowd pound bough

Did you hear /aů/ in each word above?

Make a chart like the one shown for the spellings of /aů/.
On your chart, write the four words above in separate columns.
Circle the letters that spell /aů/.
Then write these letters in the box above each word.

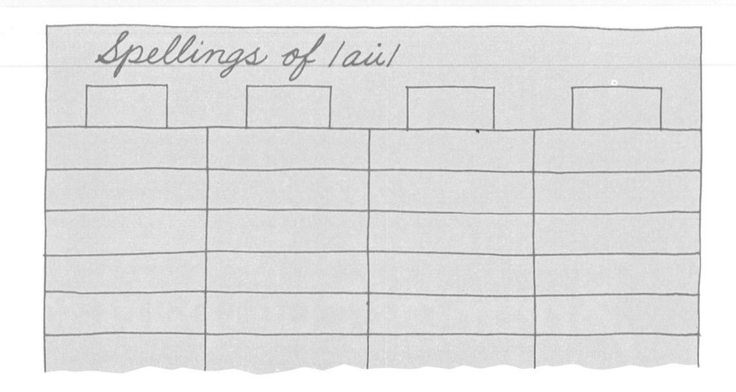

B Reread the words in the title of this section. Write all of the words containing /aů/ in the correct column of the chart. Circle the letters that spell /aů/ in each word you wrote.

C Now read the words below. If you hear /aů/ in a word, write the word in the correct column of your chart. Circle the letters that spell /aů/ in each word you wrote. Don't use any of the words that don't contain /aů/.

crown shout know about

amount now douse four

thousand court mouth down

house without snow drought

D **Extension.** Below are pronunciation codes for words containing /au̇/. Spell each word. Use a dictionary to check the spellings.

1 /prau̇d/ **2** /hau̇/ **3** /ˈtau̇-əl/ **4** /plau̇/ **5** /rau̇nd/ **6** /au̇ch/

Add these words to your chart for spellings of /au̇/.
Circle the letters that spell /au̇/ in each word you wrote.

A word history

The word *coin* has changed in meaning and spelling over many years. It began over two thousand years ago with the Roman word *cuneum* /kyu̇-ˈnē-əm/. At first, it had nothing to do with money. In the Roman language, which was Latin, the word *cuneum* meant "a wedge." The first metal money the Romans made was shaped like a wedge. So, the same word, *cuneum*, was used for the wedge-shaped metal.

About three hundred years ago, the French were using this word, spelled *coing*. It meant both something wedge-shaped, such as a corner or an angle, and the metal money.

The word came into English from the French. In English it is now used in these forms.

quoin or **coign** /kȯin/ a wedge or cornerstone
coin /kȯin/ a metal piece of money

To print the design on metal money, a wedge-shaped stamp was used. So money was coined with a wedge. Then the design on the money was spoken of as being coined. Finally the money itself became known as a coin, or metal that had been marked with a wedge-shaped stamp.

Latin	*cuneum*	wedge-shaped coin
French	*coing*	something wedge-shaped; metal money
English	*quoin* or *coign*	wedge or cornerstone
	coin	metal piece of money

Who's riding Whose bike?

The words *who's* and *whose* are homophones. They are both pronounced /hüz/.

What two words make up the contraction *who's?*

It is easier to remember how to use each of these words in a sentence if you remember that *who's* stands for *who is* or *who has*. And *whose* shows possession, so it is almost always followed by a noun.

Write the correct word, *who's* or *whose*, for each of the following sentences.

1 I wonder _____ roller skates these are.
2 I wonder _____ playing on the playground.
3 _____ going to the birthday party?
4 _____ birthday party is it?
5 She's the girl _____ such a good ball player.
6 He's the boy _____ such a great swimmer.

What's the key word?

Write the answer to each question below. In each answer, *key* will be part of the word. The first one has been done for you.

1 What key is hardest to turn? *donkey*
2 What key likes bananas?
3 What key is liked best at Thanksgiving?
4 What key is a hole in a door?

Capital letters

You know that the first word in each sentence must begin with a capital letter. Proper nouns must begin with capital letters also. A proper noun is a name of a certain person, place, or thing. When we write about mountains, we do not begin the word *mountain* with a capital letter. But when we write about the Rocky Mountains, we use capital letters for every word that is part of the name. *Rocky Mountains* is the name of a certain group of mountains.

Listed below are some kinds of proper nouns that should begin with a capital letter.

1 the name of a person or a pet, such as Victor Anderson or Blackie
2 titles of people when the titles are used as parts of their names, such as Ms. Jones or Dr. Hill
3 names of cities, states, and countries, such as Miami, Idaho, and Japan
4 names of the days of the week and the months of the year, such as Monday and November
5 names for holidays or special days, such as Halloween or Thanksgiving
6 names of groups of people, such as Orientals and Mexicans
7 names for God, such as God, Lord, and Jehovah
8 any common noun used in place of a proper noun, such as Dad or Mother

No capital letters have been used in the following paragraph. First read the paragraph. Then rewrite the paragraph correctly on a sheet of paper.

the first thanksgiving took place in 1621
it was at plymouth colony in massachusetts.
it had been a hard year for the new settlers.
so governor william bradford set aside a day
for the people to give thanks. they gave
thanks for their food, friends, and families.
they also gave thanks for their new freedom
in america. they shared the meal with
ninety indians who had helped them learn
the ways of a new land. each year, on
the fourth thursday of November, americans
still give thanks.

What is in a leaf that isn't in leaves?

A At the beginning of a word, /f/ is often spelled with the letter *f*.

Write four words that begin with /f/ spelled *f*.

B How is /f/ spelled at the end of a word? Read the following words.

half beef graph
cliff giraffe

With what sound does each word end?

Make a chart like the one shown for spellings of /f/ at the end of words. Write each of the words listed at the left in a separate column. Circle the letters that spell final /f/ in each word you wrote. Write these letters above each column. The first word has been done for you.

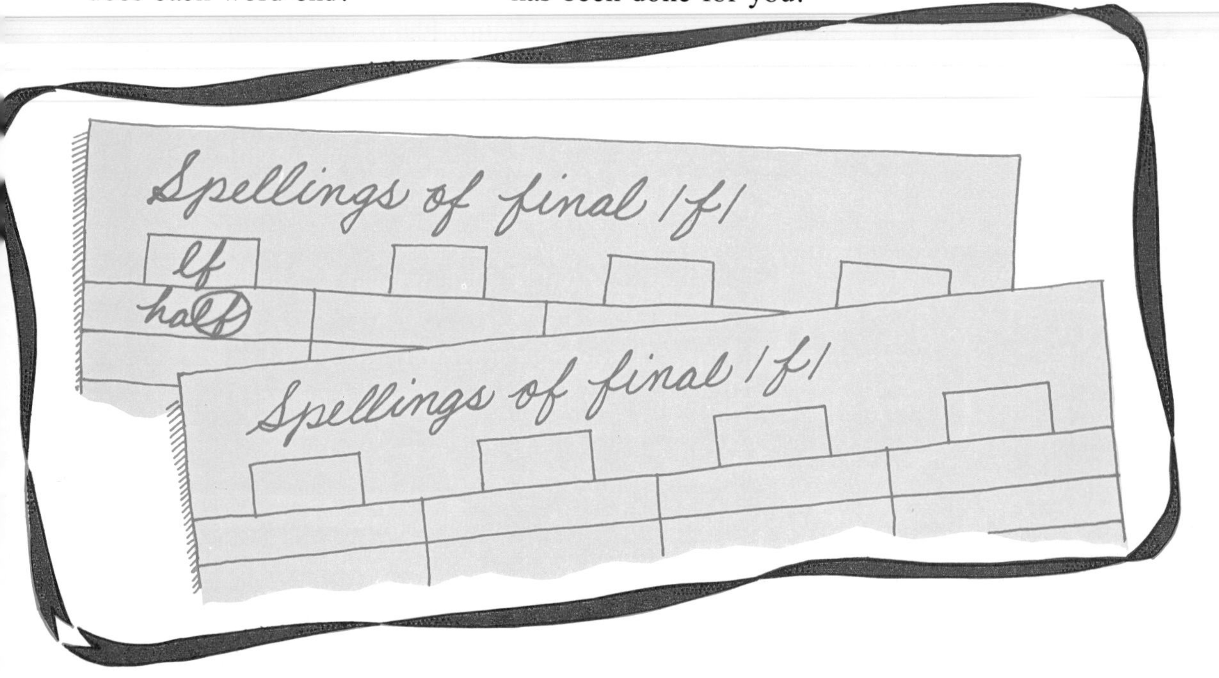

C Now say the words *laugh* and *enough*. Do you hear /f/ at the end of each word? Write *laugh* and *enough* in a new column. Circle the letters that spell /f/ and write them at the top of the column.

D Look for other words that end in /f/. Write them in the correct columns of your chart. You may need to start new columns.

Micro- + -scope = microscope

A Look at the word part **micro-.**
Why is there a hyphen after it?

Micro- is often used with
other words or word parts
to form words used in science.
Read the following definitions.

micro- means ''small''
-scope means ''an instrument
for viewing or observing''

microscope means ''an instrument
used for viewing small objects''

Add **micro-** to another word to fit the definitions
given below. The first one has been done for you.

1 an organism of very small size
microorganism

2 a very small scale

3 a very small photograph

4 film on which printed matter is
made in very small size

B Read the definition
for **-scope** again. Then read
these definitions.

stetho- means ''breast, chest''
peri- means ''all around, about''
tele- means ''at a distance''

Combine **-scope** with one of the word parts above
to fit each definition below.

1 an instrument for viewing around something

2 an instrument used to discover and study sounds
made in the body, especially in the chest

3 an instrument for viewing objects at a distance

The schwa sound

Read the following pronunciation codes.
Then write each word as it should be spelled.

1 /brəsh/ **3** /həng/ **5** /i-'nəf/ **7** /'trəb-əl/

2 /ə-'slēp/ **4** /ə-'hed/ **6** /sən/ **8** /'tik-ət/

What sound is the same
in all of the words you wrote?

Circle the letters that spell /ə/
in the words you wrote.
Can you think of other words
that have this sound?

Change a letter

This is a spelling game. It can help you to understand how important one letter in a word can be.
Read each definition below. Then supply the missing letter to make the correct word to fit each definition.

1 a _ ake: to cook in an oven
b _ ake: an inland body of water

2 a b _ g: to ask for
b b _ g: a sack
c b _ g: an insect

3 a _ ive: to plunge headfirst into water
b _ ive: one more than four
c _ ive: housing for honeybees

4 a f _ x: a wild animal
b f _ x: to mend or repair

5 a _ ole: an opening into or through something
b _ ole: an acting part

6 a hal _: one of two equal parts
b hal _: to stop

7 a stoo _: rose to one's feet
b stoo _ : a seat without back or arms

8 a _oll: to move by turning over and over
b _oll: a tax or fee paid for a right

Echoing words

A

Some words in our language are like echoes. They imitate the sound they name. Listed at right are some echoing words.

buzz
A honeybee can buzz. Can a fly buzz?
hoot
An owl can hoot. Can you hoot?
zoom
A jet can zoom. Can a race car zoom?

Write the name of an object that might make a sound like each of the echoing words listed below.

1 thump **2** crash **3** clang **4** splash **5** squeak **6** swish **7** howl **8** gurgle

B

Write an echoing word that would imitate the sound each of the objects at right might make.

1 shoes **2** donkey **3** traffic **4** storm **5** wind **6** ocean

You can write stories and poems using echoing words to imitate sounds you want to talk about. Read the poem below.

I Like Noise

I like noise
The clang of boys
The talking of girls
The bang of a drum
The pop! of a balloon of gum
The clatter and splatter
The fall of a ladder
Clinkity, clankity, clunkety,
Chattery, boompety, bumpity,
Bashity, bangity, blankety,
Bash! Bang! Clang!
Dang! Ding! Dong!
Laughter and banter
Patter and chatter
Goop, doop, joom and doom,
The crash of cars
The pop of tar
Gergoon, zoom and boom,
The clatter of toys,
That's why I LIKE NOISE!

Lance Rengel, Grade 4, Diamond Lake Schools, Illinois

What kind of animal do you find in the clouds?

12

A

Say the words *rein* and *sleigh*.
What vowel sound do you hear in these words?

Write each word.
Then circle the letters
that spell the vowel sound in each word.

You will want to add these words to your chart
for spellings of /ā/ if you don't already have them.

B

Read the definitions for *rain* and *rein*.
Then write a sentence using the word *rain*
and a sentence using the word *rein*.

rain /rān/ water falling in drops from the clouds
rein /rān/ a line fastened to a bit by which a rider or driver controls an animal

C

1 What is the homophone of *dear* that means "an animal"?

2 Now, to answer the riddle in the title of this section, write the compound word for an antlered animal found in the north that pulls a sleigh.
What kind of animal do you find in the clouds?

3 What is the first syllable in *reindeer?*

4 What is the homophone of *rein* that means "water falling from the clouds"?

5 What is the second syllable in *reindeer?*

6 What is the homophone of *deer* that means "a loved one"?

7 Now, use the answers to questions 4 and 6 to answer the riddle. What kind of animal do you find in the clouds?

/f/ as in Phone

A Read the following words.
Listen to the sound that is the same
in all the words.

photo elephant
paragraph photograph

1 What sound is the same in all of the words?

2 What letters spell that sound?

3 In what part of a word do you find the spelling for that sound?

B English words that have /f/ spelled *ph*
come from the ancient Greek language. One word part
taken from ancient Greek is **-phone,** meaning "sound."
It can be added to the end of other words or word parts
to form many words. One example is *homophone*.
Homo- means "the same" or "alike." **-Phone** means sound. *Homophone* means
words that sound alike.

Another word part, spelled **phon-** or **phono-**, also means "sound."
This word part can be added to the beginning of other words or word parts
to form many words, too. An example is *phonic*. **Phon-** means "sound"
and **-ic** means "related to." *Phonic* means "related to or making sound."

Write three words that have **-phone, phon-,** or **phono-** in them.
Then, beside each word you wrote, explain what its meaning
has to do with sound.

C Write the words at right.
Circle the letter or letters
that spell /f/ in each word.

phone	laugh	alphabet
puff	beef	enough
knife	tough	giraffe
elephant	safe	leaf

Memory tricks

A memory trick helps you remember how a word should be spelled. If you have trouble spelling a certain word, sometimes a trick can help you remember how it is spelled. Read these examples.

Word	**Memory trick**
hear	I *hear* with my *ear*.
meat	I *eat meat*.
meet	You gr*ee*t those you m*ee*t.
together	We'll go *together to get her* a present.
highway	The *highway* is so *high way* up there.
breakfast	We'll make a *break fast* after *breakfast*.
anyway	*Anyway*, we can't find *any way* out of here.

Can you make up other memory tricks to help you remember how to spell some words?

Proofreading for spelling

Proofread means "to look for mistakes." Read the following paragraph all the way through. Then proofread it for words that are not spelled correctly. Write the correct spelling for each misspelled word. Use a dictionary if you are not sure of the spelling. Then rewrite the entire paragraph correctly.

It is saff to say that the elefant has the longest knows. His ears are large, to. But wen there is a contest for the longest nek, the elefant loses. The giraf has the longest nek. He has enuf nek for three elefants. Wouldn't you laff if you saw that long nose and long nek togeter? Can you picture them on the same animal? What wood you call such an animal? Would it be an eleraffe or a giraphant?

Merry mix-up

Read the clues and unscramble the words to complete the puzzle.

Down

1 ROLCAS: songs sung at Christmastime

2 SBLLE: they make a jingling noise on a sleigh

4 SHRTIAMSC: when Santa comes

5 GEHSIL: what Santa rides in

7 VESEL: Santa's helpers

9 ILHOADY: a special day, such as Christmas

11 ARSTS: things shining in the sky at night

Across

3 TLNSACASUA: driver of the Christmas sleigh

6 LEDCNA: something that burns

8 EDRIENRE: Rudolph, the rednosed ____

10 FIGST: things we give

12 EERT: gifts are placed under it

13 LITSGH: something used to decorate Christmas trees

14 NSWO: makes a white Christmas

/ü/ as in Shoot for the Moon

13

A Say the words at the right.
Listen to the vowel sound
that is the same in all of them.

move noon
grew fruit through

Do you hear /ü/? Make a chart like the one shown.
Write each of the words listed above
in a separate column on your chart. Circle the letters
that spell /ü/. Then write the letters you circled in the box at the top
of each column. The first word has been done for you.

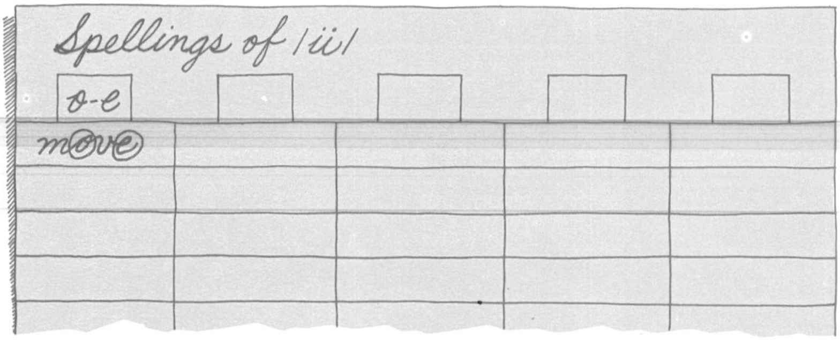

Spellings of /ü/

o-e				
move				

B Say the words *suit, whose, shoot,* and *threw*.
How is /ü/ spelled in each word? Write each word
in the correct column on your chart.
Circle the letters that spell /ü/.

C Listed below are pronunciation codes
for six words. Spell the correct word for each code.
Check your Spelling Dictionary to see if you have spelled
the words correctly.

1 /drü/
2 /spün/
3 /tüth/
4 /zü/
5 /ˈmü-vē/
6 /kül/

Add these words to your chart.
Look for other words that have /ü/ and write
each in the correct column on your chart.
You may have to begin new columns.

From adjective to adverb

A The word *quick*
is usually an adjective.
It says something
about a noun.
Read the following sentence.

The rabbit was quick.

You can form an adverb by adding
the suffix **-ly** to the base word *quick*.
An adverb says something about a verb.
Read the sentence below.

The rabbit turned quickly and hopped away.

The following base words can be used as adjectives.
Add the suffix **-ly** to each adjective to form an adverb.

1 careful **2** loose **3** soft **4** free
5 bright **6** brave **7** quiet **8** slow

Did you have to make
any spelling changes in the base words when you added **-ly?**

B Now look at the following pairs of words.
busy — busily easy — easily

What was done to the spelling of the adjective
in order to form the adverb?

Pattern:

To form an adverb,
add **-ly** to a base word
that is an adjective.
sad — sadly cold — coldly
sly — slyly

Pattern:

If a base word ends with *y*
and has more than one syllable,
change *y* to *i* and add **-ly.**
sleepy — sleepily happy — happily
hungry — hungrily

Listed below are more adjectives.
Add **-ly** to each adjective to form an adverb.

1 sure **2** pretty **3** angry **4** dry
5 loud **6** merry **7** lone **8** easy

Possessive forms of nouns

A Read the following sentence.

The boy's dog was seen in the park.

1 Which word is in the possessive form?
2 Does the dog belong to one boy or more than one boy?
3 How can you tell?

B Now, read the next sentence.

The boys' dog was seen in the park.

1 Does the dog belong to one boy or more than one boy?
2 How can you tell?

Read the following examples of the possessive forms of singular nouns and plural nouns.

a dog's food — two dogs' food

a lion's cubs — two lions' cubs

one farmer's fields — four farmers' fields

C What do you do to form the possessive of a plural noun that does not end in *s*? Add an apostrophe and an *s ('s)*. Read the following examples.

the children's pet
the men's lunches
the sheep's pen
the geese's feeding grounds

Complete the following rules for writing possessive forms of nouns.

1 For singular nouns, always add ____. a princess's crown

2 For plural nouns not ending in *s*, add ____. women's meeting

3 For plural nouns ending in *s*, just add ____. girls' bicycles

D Write a sentence using each of the following nouns in the possessive form.

1 geese
2 Joe
3 teachers
4 fox
5 ladies
6 mice
7 monkey
8 buses
9 neighbor

As busy as a juggler with poison ivy

A You can often use comparisons to make what you have to say more interesting or more clear. Did you ever think of a train the way Rowena Bennett does in the following poem?

A Modern Dragon

A train is a dragon that roars through the dark.
He wriggles his tail as he sends up a spark.
He pierces the night with his one yellow eye,
And all the earth trembles when he rushes by.

"A Modern Dragon" from
Songs From Around a Toadstool Table by Rowena Bennett.

Of course, the poet didn't really mean that the train was a dragon. She's telling us how a train is like a dragon.

B Sometimes you can use the words *like* or *as* to show a comparison.

> Matthew spoke in a voice *like* the roar of thunder.
> Evening was as quiet *as* a blade of waving grass.

Suppose you wanted to tell about something sticky, like melted chocolate. What could you compare it to? Think of the stickiest thing you know.

> Melted chocolate is as sticky as warm chewing gum.
>
> Melted chocolate is as sticky as spilled honey.
>
> Melted chocolate is as sticky as the inside of Scotch tape.

C Below are some ideas for you to write about. Write a sentence making a comparison for each idea.

1 . . . felt like . . .
2 . . . ran like . . .
3 . . . as slippery as . . .
4 . . . as bumpy as . . .
5 . . . as noisy as . . .
6 . . . as quiet as . . .
7 . . . as easy as . . .
8 . . . sounded like . . .
9 . . . looked like . . .
10 . . . jumped like . . .

/ər/ as in the Early Bird gets the Worm 14

A Say the following words.

1 work **2** perch **3** sturdy **4** butter **5** sir **6** thirty **7** sugar **8** either **9** nurse **10** her **11** person **12** forgive

Did you hear /ər/ in all of the above words?

Write the letters that spell /ər/ in each word.

B Now, say the following words.

learn

earth

pearl

What sound is the same in these three words?

How is that sound spelled in each word?

C Look at the pronunciation codes for the words below. Write the correct spelling of each word. Circle the letters that spell /ər/ in each word you write.

1 /ˈdrī-vər/ **2** /sər-ˈprīz/

3 /ˈspīd-ər/ **4** /ərth/

5 /wərm/ **6** /ˈfärm-ər/

7 /ˈtər-kē/ **8** /ˈər-lē/

9 /shərt/ **10** /ˈsil-vər/

Check each word in your Spelling Dictionary to be sure you spelled it correctly.

In Unit 7, you began a chart for spellings of /ər/. Add the words in this section to the correct columns of your chart. You may already have some of the words listed.

Who can raise things without lifting them?

A Read the following sentences.

He *farms* in Iowa.
He is a good *farmer*.

In the first sentence,
is the word *farms*
used as a noun or as a verb?

In the second sentence,
is the word *farmer* used as a noun or as a verb?

B Nouns can be formed by adding the suffix **-er** to base forms of verbs.
Read the following examples.

noun		*verb*
A rider is a person who rides.		

noun		*verb*
A shopper is a person who shops.		

There are three spelling patterns to follow for adding **-er** to verbs
to form nouns. Read the following examples showing these patterns.

Pattern 1:	Pattern 2:	Pattern 3:
hike — hiker	swim — swimmer	teach — teacher
skate — skater	trap — trapper	dream — dreamer
move — mover	plan — planner	play — player

1 In Pattern 1, the base words
all end with *e*. What was done
to the base words before adding **-er?**

2 In Pattern 2, the base words end
in a single consonant with a simple vowel sound
before the consonant. What was done
to the base words before adding **-er?**

3 Most other base words follow Pattern 3.
What was done to the base words
in Pattern 3 before adding **-er?**

C Make each verb into a noun. You may want to check
a dictionary after you have finished writing each noun.

1 bake **2** catch **3** plan **4** trap **5** lead
6 pack **7** rule **8** work **9** win **10** trade

If side by side, divide!

Say each of the following words.

butter bullet
cotton

How many vowel sounds do you hear in each word?

How many syllables does each word have?

B Sometimes you may run out of space at the end of a writing line. Then you may have to divide a word at a syllable division. You would write part of the word, put a hyphen after it, and then write the rest of the word on the next line. You have probably seen words divided in things you have read.

Where would you divide *butter, cotton,* and *bullet* at the end of a line of writing? Look at the divisions below.

but · ter   cot · ton   bul · let

Write *butter, cotton,* and *bullet* as they are shown above.

Put a V over each vowel in *butter*.
Put a C over each of the middle consonants.
Do the same with *cotton* and *bullet*.

Where is a word divided when double consonants come between two vowels?

Does the second syllable in each word begin with a vowel or a consonant?

C Rewrite each of the following words. Mark these words with VCCV as you did the words *butter, cotton*, and *bullet* in Part B. Then draw a line to divide each word into syllables. The first one has been done for you.

1 coffee   vccv coffee

2 follow

3 marry

4 sunny

5 penny

6 rubber

7 cottage

8 hurry

When you have finished, check each word in your Spelling Dictionary. Check the syllable divisions of the entry words.

Consonant capers

A Read the following groups of words and sentences.

1 good golly gumdrops

2 one merry Monday morning

3 proud Prince Paul

4 The sun sank slowly.

5 Bertha bounced Billy's blue ball.

6 Sally sells seashells at the seashore.

What did you notice about the beginning consonant sounds in each group of words?

Rewrite each group of words. Then circle the beginning consonant letters that spell the sound or sounds that are repeated. For example, circle the *g*'s that spell /g/ in each word of the first group of words.

B Writers sometimes use words that repeat sounds. Read the poem.

The Early Evening

The bees began buzzing
When the black bull bellowed.
A friendly fox feasted,
    forgetting to look about
As the forget-me-not flowers flowed
    in the gentle breeze.
And we enjoyed entirely
    these early evening hours.

Now write two consonant capers of your own. Make them at least two lines long.

Adding -y to nouns to show what kind 15

A Read the following sentences.

> The cowboys traveled a trail that was covered with *dust*.
> The cowboys traveled a *dusty* trail.

1 In the first sentence,
is the word *dust* a noun or an adjective?

2 In the second sentence,
is the word *dusty* a noun or an adjective?

When the suffix **-y** is added to a noun,
the new word is usually an adjective.

B Read the following examples of spelling patterns.

Pattern 1:	Pattern 2:
rose — rosy	sun — sunny
lace — lacy	knot — knotty
fleece — fleecy	chop — choppy
slime — slimy	tin — tinny

Pattern 3:

hand — handy
luck — lucky
silver — silvery
hill — hilly

Write phrases using the nouns at the right as adjectives. Change each noun to an adjective by adding **-y.** The first one has been done for you.

1 sun *a sunny Saturday*

2 bone **3** sleep

4 bump **5** rain

6 ice **7** dirt

8 fun **9** silk

10 mud **11** mess

12 leaf **13** rock

14 snow

One or more?

A Look at these two spelling patterns for forming plural words.

dollar — dollars	
tip — tips	coal — coals

dress — dresses	
box — boxes	crutch — crutches

A word to which **-s** or **-es** has been added to show that it means more than one is a *plural* word. Add five plural words to each spelling pattern below.

-s	**-es**
dollars	dresses

B There are some plural words that are formed without **-s** or **-es.** Read the following example.

His foot is sore.
His feet are sore.

What is the plural form of *foot?*

Write the plural form of each underlined word in the sentences below.

1 Our cat hunted for the mouse.

2 Dave has a lucky lion's tooth.

3 The new principal is a woman.

4 Ask this child where he lives.

5 Conrad's brother is a policeman.

6 The goose chased the cat away.

More side-by-side division

A Say each of the words below and listen to the number of syllables each word has. Rewrite each word. Put a C over each of the two consonant letters that come between vowels in each word. Then put a V over the vowel letter that comes before two consonants and a V over the vowel letter that comes after two consonants.

silver engine farmer

Are the two consonants alike or not alike?

How would you divide *silver, engine,* and *farmer* at the end of a line of writing? Look at the divisions below.

VC CV	VC CV	VC CV
s i l | v e r	e n | g i n e	f a r | m e r

Where is each word divided?

B Rewrite each word below. Put a C over each of the two consonant letters that come between vowels in each word. Then put a V over the vowel letter that comes before two consonants and a V over the vowel letter that comes after two consonants. Then draw a line to divide the word into syllables.

1 enjoy **2** until

3 compare **4** listen

5 often **6** picnic

Pen pals

A The letter on page 61 is a sample of a friendly letter. The five main parts of a friendly letter are labeled. In the body of the letter, Brad has done two important things. He has given Chris news about himself, and he has shown interest in what his friend is doing.

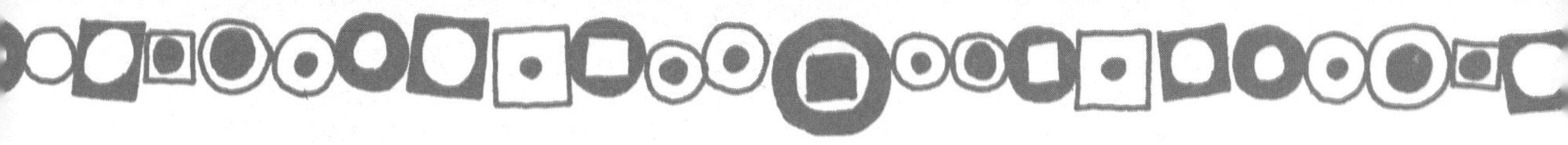

B Answer each of the following questions about the letter. Choose your answers from the words listed just below. You will have to use some of the words more than once, and you will not need some of them at all.

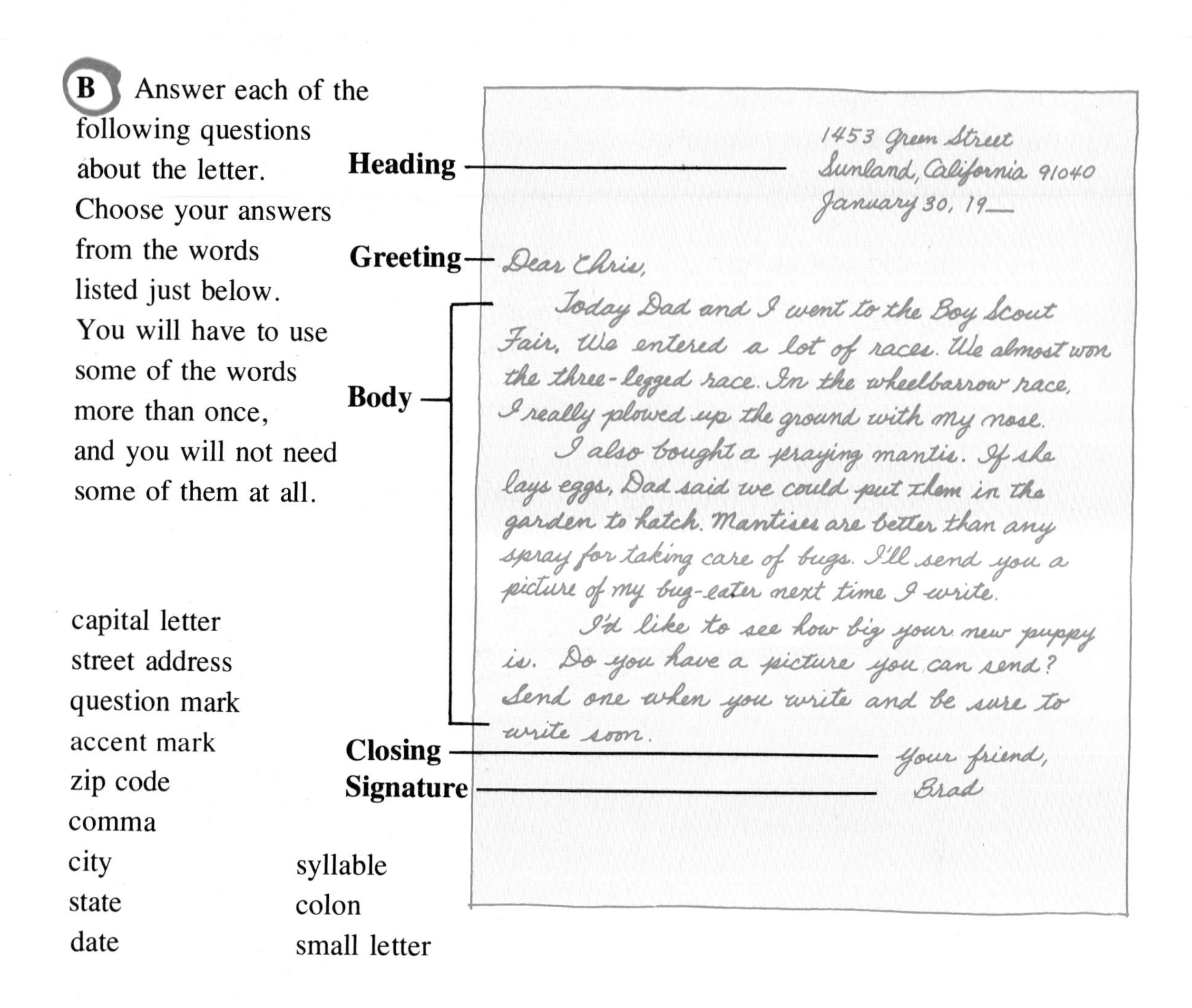

1453 Green Street
Sunland, California 91040
January 30, 19—

Dear Chris,

Today Dad and I went to the Boy Scout Fair. We entered a lot of races. We almost won the three-legged race. In the wheelbarrow race, I really plowed up the ground with my nose.

I also bought a praying mantis. If she lays eggs, Dad said we could put them in the garden to hatch. Mantises are better than any spray for taking care of bugs. I'll send you a picture of my bug-eater next time I write.

I'd like to see how big your new puppy is. Do you have a picture you can send? Send one when you write and be sure to write soon.

Your friend,
Brad

capital letter
street address
question mark
accent mark
zip code
comma
city
state
date
syllable
colon
small letter

1 What five things does the heading have?
2 With what kind of punctuation mark does the greeting end?
3 With what kind of letter,
capital or small, does the first word in the closing begin?
With what kind of letter does the second word in the closing begin?
4 With what kind of punctuation mark does the closing end?

C Write a letter to someone who has moved or to a friend. Tell what you have been doing. Also ask about some of the things your friend might be doing. Make sure you use all the parts of a friendly letter.

Consonant Clusters

16

A Do you know what a cluster is? You can talk about a cluster of roses, a cluster of grapes, or a cluster of people. A cluster is a bunch or a set of things close together.

What do you suppose a consonant cluster is?

A *consonant cluster* is a bunch of consonant letters set close together. Below are some words with consonant clusters. Say the words. Notice that the beginning consonant sounds are all spoken, yet they blend together.

*bl*ue *fr*y *dr*aw *gl*ass

*tr*eat *pl*an *cl*ub *str*ing

A good blender is *s*. Use your Spelling Dictionary to see how many different consonant clusters you can find that begin with *s*.

B Make a list of consonant clusters. Write ten different consonant clusters that begin with *s*. Write an example word for each cluster. The first one has been started for you. (Do not include *sh* in your list because it spells a single sound.)

Consonant Clusters Beginning With *s*

cluster	word
sc	

Noun substitutes

A Read the two sentences below. Notice the subject of each sentence

Dan likes to write.

He wrote that poem.

You can use a noun substitute, such as *he, she,* or *it,* instead of repeating a noun. These noun substitutes are called *pronouns*. Pronouns refer to a noun that has been mentioned.

In the sentence "He wrote that poem," who does the word *he* refer to?

B Some pronouns do not refer to any certain noun.
If you found a penny on the playground, you might say

Somebody lost a penny.

The pronoun *somebody* does not refer to any certain person. It refers to an unknown or unnamed person.

Twelve pronouns can be formed by using the following words.

Each pronoun has one of these as a beginning.
some any every no

Each pronoun has one of these as an ending.
body one thing

C Make a chart like the one shown.
In the first column of the chart, add the words *some, any, every,* and *no* to **-body** to form pronouns.

In the second column, add the words *some, any, every,* and *no* to **-thing**. Do you say the word *nothing* the way you would say the words *no thing?*

In the third column, add the words *some, any, every,* and *no* to **-one**. (Be careful. One of these combinations is spelled as two words.)

-body	-thing	-one

Now, how many pronouns do you have in your chart?

Look and listen before you divide!

A If a word contains a VCCV pattern you have learned to divide the word between the two consonants. The middle consonants can be alike or not alike. Use what you have learned to divide the following words into syllables. Write each word. Then draw a line to show where each word should be divided.

sudden doctor worry

B Now say these words. Listen to the single sound the underlined consonants spell.

change show bath rock

Each pair of underlined consonants is a *digraph*. A digraph is two letters that spell a single sound. Since a digraph stands for a single sound, you never divide a word between the letters of a digraph. For example, look at the following words.

moth | er fa | ther

What consonant digraph appears in both words?

Are the words divided into syllables between the letters in the digraphs?

In which syllable does the digraph appear in *mother?*

In which syllable does the digraph appear in *father?*

C Say the words below. Rewrite each word and circle the consonant digraph. Use your Spelling Dictionary to find out where to divide each word into syllables. Then draw a line between the syllables in each word. The first word has been marked for you.

1 telephone *tele|phone*
2 others
3 pocket
4 everything
5 nothing
6 either
7 fashion
8 clothing
9 rocket
10 somewhere
11 awhile
12 rather

In the exercise you just completed,
why didn't you divide between the digraphs?

What should be added to the rule for dividing words
with a VCCV pattern into syllables?

When two consonant letters come between two vowel letters, divide between the two consonants unless ____.

Envelope examination

Look at the model of an envelope below.

return address ____ Brad Craig
1453 Green Street
Sunland, California 91040

stamp ____

address ____ Chris Storm
1760 Windfall Road
Morton Grove, Illinois 60053

1 Whose address is written
in the upper left corner, the sender's or the receiver's?

2 Why is a return address needed?

3 What is in the return address?

4 Where do you find a comma in the return address?

5 Whose address is in the center
of the envelope, the sender's or the receiver's?

6 Is there any difference in the kind of information used in this address?

7 Is there any difference in punctuation of the two addresses?

Address an envelope for the letter you wrote in Unit 15.
Don't forget your return address.

Special verb forms 17

A The following sentences show three forms of the verb *remember*.

Present form: Doctors remember many people.
Present **-s** form: Doctor Brown remembers many people.
Past form: Dr. Brown remembered many people.

Write the correct forms of each verb given below. The first one has been done for you.

Present Form	Present **-s** Form	Past Form
1 I burn	he burns	he burned

2 they report **3** we dress **4** I watch **5** we raise

6 they chase **7** you study **8** they worry

B Below are some irregular verbs. These verbs are called irregular because the past form is not made in the regular way, that is by adding **-ed.** Compare the two forms of each verb.

ride — rode	hang — hung
dig — dug	bite — bit
hold — held	ring — rang

What changes to make the past form, the vowel sound or the consonant sounds?

For each sentence below, write the past form of the verb in parentheses following the sentence.

1 We ____ holes in the sand. (dig)

2 Victor and Leroy ____ their jackets. (hang)

3 The bell ____ at nine o'clock. (rings)

4 The monkeys ____ animal crackers. (eat)

5 Angie ____ home on the bus. (rides)

6 She ____ the little puppy. (holds)

In what month do people talk the least?

A Say the following words.

/ˈjan-yə-ˌwer-ē/
/ˈfeb-rə-ˌwer-ē/

How many syllables does each word have?

The second word can be tricky to spell, because many people do not pronounce the *r* in the second syllable.

Spell the two words given in the pronunciation codes above.

Why does each word begin with a capital letter?

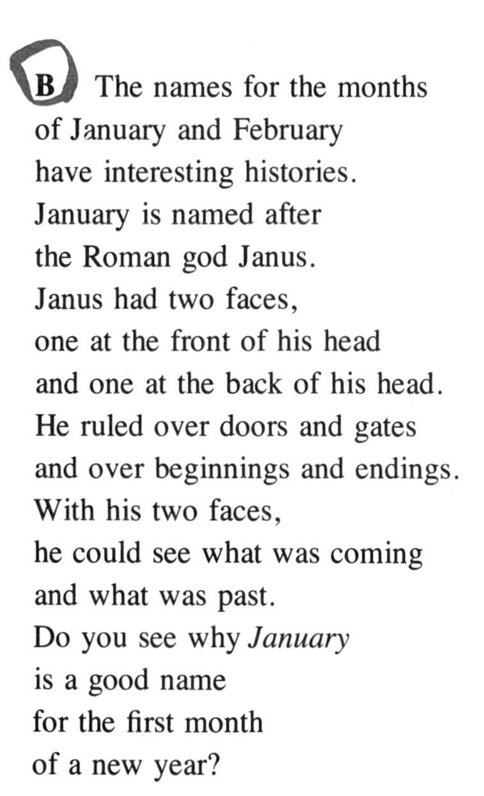

B The names for the months of January and February have interesting histories. January is named after the Roman god Janus. Janus had two faces, one at the front of his head and one at the back of his head. He ruled over doors and gates and over beginnings and endings. With his two faces, he could see what was coming and what was past. Do you see why *January* is a good name for the first month of a new year?

The name February comes from the Latin word *februare* meaning "to make pure." In the early Roman calendar, February was the twelfth month of the year. During this month the Romans made themselves pure to get ready for the new year. So they called the month *Februarius*. It was Julius Caesar, an ancient Roman ruler, who made February the second month of the year.

More about syllables

A You have learned how a word is usually divided into syllables when it contains a VCCV pattern, as in *happy*.

VC CV
hap•py

Now look at the letter pattern
in the words *Friday* and *Saturday*.

V CV	VC V
Fri·day	**Sat·ur·day**

In the VCV pattern, the first vowel is followed by a single ____.

Where does the first syllable end in Friday?

Where does the first syllable end in Saturday?

Words that have a VCV pattern may be divided as follows:

1 before the consonant, as in *Friday*

2 after the consonant, as in *Saturday*

B Vowel sounds in words may sometimes be a clue to how the word should be divided into syllables. The first vowel sound in Friday is /ī/. This sound and /ā/, /ē/, /ō/, and /yü/ are sounds that are the same as their letter names.

Is the first vowel sound in *Saturday* one of these vowel sounds?

Here is an idea that often works when you need to divide a word containing a VCV pattern:

If the first vowel sounds like its name, divide after that vowel.

If the first vowel doesn't sound like its name, divide after the consonant.

Now rewrite each of the words below.
Then mark the VCV pattern over each of the words. Say each word.
Draw a line between where you think the first syllable ends
and the second syllable begins.

1 wagon **2** study **3** broken **4** spider **5** family

6 finish **7** hotel **8** agent **9** November **10** recess

Check your Spelling Dictionary
to see if you divided the words into syllables correctly.

Famous February figures

Our first president, George Washington, was born on February 22.
Abraham Lincoln, the sixteenth president, was born on February 12.
Both men are among the greatest our country has known.
We've honored these presidents in many different ways.
Cities, streets, schools, and parks have been named for them.
We celebrate their birthdays each February.

Choose one of these men to learn more about.
Look for information in an encyclopedia
or ask a librarian to help you find a book about him.

Write an outline for a report, listing the things you want to try
to find out. The following is an example of an outline.

I. The person
   A. His birthdate
   B. Brief description of him
   C. His family
   D. His education
   E. Important facts
      about his early life
II. The kind of person he was
   A. What kind of work he did
   B. What he liked to do for fun
III. What he did to become famous
   A. Before he became president
   B. While he was president
IV. His death

Use your outline as a guide.
Find as much information as you can about each topic in your outline.
Start a new paragraph for each main heading.
After you write your report, reread it to check for spelling
and other errors before you turn it in to your teacher.

More homophone hang-ups 18

Homophones like *stare* and *stair* can sometimes cause spelling problems. Homophones sound the same even though they have different meanings and different spellings.

Here is a homophone game. Each pronunciation code has at least two homophones. With each pronunciation, you are given the meanings of the homophones. First, say the word. Then, write the spelling that goes with each meaning.

1 /tü/
- **a** one more than one
- **b** toward
- **c** also

2 /tāl/
- **a** a story
- **b** part of an animal's body

3 /blü/
- **a** a color
- **b** past form of *blow*

4 /bēt/
- **a** a vegetable
- **b** to mix by stirring

5 /sāl/
- **a** part on a boat that catches the wind
- **b** an exchange of goods for money

6 /sō/
- **a** to work with needle and thread
- **b** in that way

7 /hüz/
- **a** belonging to whom
- **b** contraction for *who is*

8 /thrü/
- **a** past form of *throw*
- **b** into at one side and out of the other side of

Dividing compound words

A Say the word *maybe*.
How many vowel sounds do you hear?
There is a syllable for each pronounced vowel
in a word. How many syllables does the word *maybe* have?

A compound word is made up of two
or more words. How many words are there in *maybe?*

Read the following examples of compound words.

may + be = maybe   air + port = airport   in + side = inside

How many syllables does each of the above words have?

B Dictionaries show
where words are divided
into syllables. Some dictionaries
have extra space
between the syllables in a word.
Other dictionaries have dots
between the syllables in a word.

may be   may · be

Find the entry words for the following compound words
in your Spelling Dictionary. Write each one
just the way you see it in your Spelling Dictionary.

1 without	**3** bedroom	**5** upstairs	**7** playground
2 daylight	**4** fireplace	**6** baseball	**8** somewhere

What did you discover about dividing compound words into syllables?

What letter is never found in the alphabet?

Make four columns on a piece of paper. Number the columns
1, 2, 3, and 4. Then put the words from column 1 below in alphabetical order
in column 1 on your paper. Do columns 2, 3, and 4 the same way.

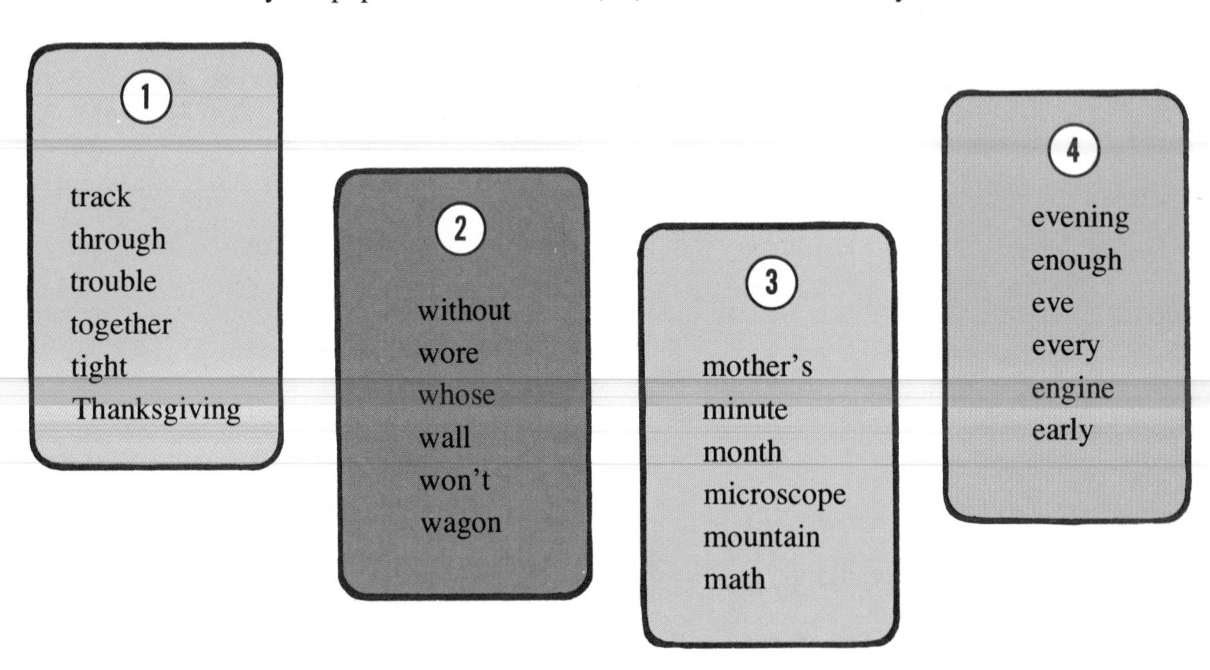

A word history

About seven hundred years ago, the only people who spoke English
were those people who lived in England. At that time,
the word *will* was spelled *woll* and pronounced /wōl/.
So, instead of saying *will not* people said *woll not*.

The contraction of the words *woll not* probably began as *woln't*.
But if you try to say *woln't*, you'll understand
why the *l* could easily drop out of the pronunciation,
leaving the contraction *won't*.

In Modern English, we still use
the contraction *won't*, although it now stands for *will* + *not*.
Write two sentences using the contraction *won't*.

Password

To find the password, write the correct word
for each meaning below. All of the words can be found in your spelling list
for this unit and in your Spelling Dictionary.

1 to think of again

2 a large antlered deer

3 contraction of *will not*

4 the first month of the year

5 past of *throw*

6 an instrument used to see
an extremely small object

1
2
3
4
5
6

When you have completed the puzzle,
the letters in the circles will spell a word
that means a small unit of time. What is the password?

Idea shop

Have you ever wished you could create a special place
where you could go when you were sad or angry? What would it be like?

Have you ever wished you were a president
or a king or a queen? What would be the first
thing you would do? Then what would you do?
What would you do on your day off?

Have you ever wanted
to find a buried treasure?
How would you find it?
What would it be?
What would you do with it?

Have you ever wanted an
unusual pet? What would
it be? What would
you name it?
Describe it.

Have you ever
wanted to
start walking
down a road
just to see
where it goes?
Where do you think
it might lead you?
What might happen?

Choose one of the ideas above to write a story or poem about,
or you may write about an idea of your own.

Y wonder

19

A The letter *y* is used to spell /y/ in words like *yellow* and *year*. It may also be used to spell some vowel sounds. Say the following words. Listen for four sounds spelled with *y*.

*y*ou m*y* m*y*ster*y*

In which of the above words does *y* spell a consonant sound?

In which of the above words does *y* spell a vowel sound?

What three different vowel sounds does *y* spell in the words listed above?

B Make a chart like the one shown for sounds spelled with *y*.

Each of the words at the right has *y* in it. Say each word and decide what sound the *y* spells. Then write each word in the correct column of the chart.

marry	yet	yes	yard
February	study	physical	reply
young	bicycle	dry	system
gym	January	fairy	fry
spy	July	you'll	thirty

Sounds spelled with y

/y/	/ī/	/ē/	/i/

C Find other words with /y/, /ī/, /ē/, and /i/ spelled with *y*. You can find them in your reader, a magazine, or a dictionary. Put the words you find in the correct column on your chart.

Practice makes perfect

A You have learned the following patterns
that can help you divide written words into syllables.

1 When a word has only one vowel sound, it cannot be divided.

mouth **care** **yard**

2 When two consonants come between two vowels,
divide between the two consonants unless they form a digraph.

VC CV	VC CV	VC CV	VCC V	V CCV
mon•key	**but•ton**	**thir•ty**	**wash•ing**	**tel•e•phone**

3 When one consonant is between two vowels
and the first vowel sounds like its name, divide before the consonant.
If the first vowel doesn't sound like its name, divide after the consonant.

V CV	V CV	V CV	VC V	VC V	VC V
fa•mous	**No•vem•ber**	**spi•der**	**wag•on**	**fin•ish**	**stud•y**

4 Compound words are divided between the two words that form the compound.

play•ground **up•stairs** **day•light**

B Use the patterns in Part A
to help you divide the words below into syllables.
Write each word. Beside each word, write the number
of the pattern that applies to the division.
Then, draw a line between the letters
where the word would be divided. The first one
has been done for you.

1 marry *2 mar|ry*
2 highway
3 bow
4 vacation
5 awhile
6 raise
7 wrong
8 engine
9 sudden
10 tiny
11 airplane
12 butter
13 somewhere
14 honey

Check the syllable divisions
in your Spelling Dictionary.

Share a Pear with a Bear

A Read the following words.
Listen to the sounds
spelled with the underlined
letters of each word.

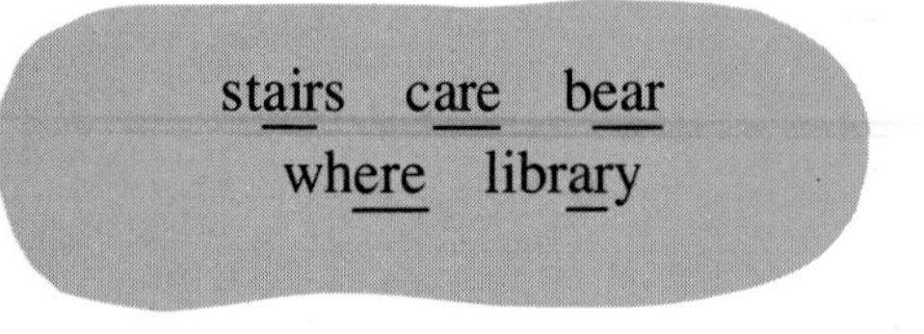

Do the underlined letters
spell the same sounds
in each word?

To some people there is a little difference in some of the sounds.
The sound code for the underlined letters in *stairs* and *bear* is /aər/.
The sound code for the underlined letters in *care* and *where* is /eər/.
The sound code for the underlined letters in *library* is /er/.

But to many people these three codes represent the same sound.
And sometimes the same letters can spell more than one of these codes.
For example, *ere* can spell /aər/ or /eər/. So, the chart for this section
will have all three sound codes on it to make the spellings easier
to understand and remember. These codes will be treated as one sound.

Make a chart like the one below to show
the different spellings of /aər/, /eər/, and /er/.
Write *stairs, care, bear, where,* and *library*
in the correct columns on your chart.
Circle the letters that spell the sounds.
The first one has been done for you.

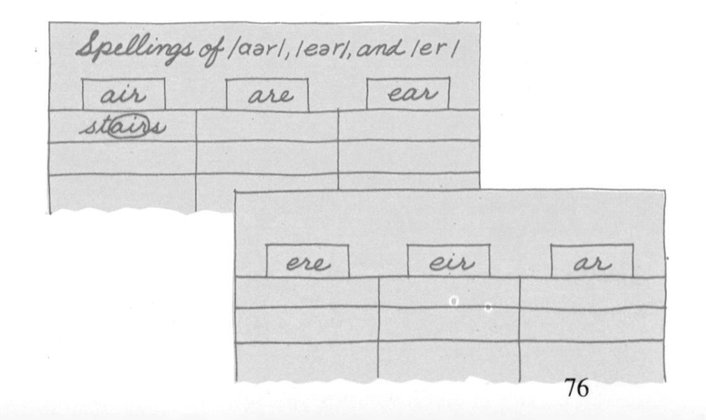

B Say the
following words.

Write each
of the words
in the correct column
on your chart.
Circle the letters
that spell /aər/,
/eər/, or /er/.

C The names of two months of the year have /er/ in their pronunciations.
Write the names in the correct column.
Circle the letters that spell that sound.

D **Extension.** Read the following pronunciations.
Write each word as it should be spelled. Some of the words are homophones. For the homophones, there is more than one word that has the same pronunciation. Use the possible spellings from your chart and a dictionary to find the homophones. The first one has been done for you.

1 /paər/ *pear, pair, pare*
2 /faər/
3 /staər/
4 /taər/
5 /ˈfaər-ē/
6 /hweər/
7 /skeər/
8 /cheər/
9 /waər/
10 /ˈlī-ˌbrer-ē/

Check the spellings of the words in a dictionary. (The dictionary may not use the same sound codes as your Spelling Dictionary uses.)
Add these words to your chart for spellings of /aər/, /eər/, and /er/.
You should already have some of them.

E Find other words that have /aər/, /eər/, or /er/.
You can look in your reader or in a dictionary.
Put the words you find in the correct columns on your chart.

Giant George Juggles Jelly beans

A Does *g* always stand for /g/, as in *goat?*
Say the words in the title.
What sound do you hear
at the beginning of each word?

What two letters
can spell that sound?

B Make a chart with one column headed "/j/ spelled *j*," one column headed "/j/ spelled *g*," and one column headed "/g/ spelled *g*." Read each word at the right. Decide if it has /j/ spelled *j*, as in *jet*, /j/ spelled *g*, as in *George*, or /g/ spelled *g*, as in *goat*. Write each word in the correct column on the chart.

gate	agent	magic
juggle	gym	finger
sugar	give	job
gem	jam	gold
jelly	gypsy	jet
league	gentle	jump

Can you think of some other words
to add to your chart? See if you can find some more words
in your reader or another book.

/ů/ as in Could a Wolf Cook?

A Say the following words.

bush couldn't
wooden woman

What vowel sound
is the same in all of these words?

How is that sound
spelled in each word?

B Below are pronunciation codes for words that have /ů/. Write each word as it should be spelled. Then make a chart like the one shown. Write each word in the correct column of your chart according to the spelling of /ů/ in the word. The first one has been done for you.

1 /pu̇t/ *put*	**4** /stu̇d/	**7** /shu̇d/	**10** /gu̇d/
2 /pu̇l/	**5** /wu̇d/	**8** /wu̇lf/	**11** /ku̇k/
3 /ˈbu̇l-ət/	**6** /tu̇k/	**9** /ku̇d/	**12** /hu̇k/

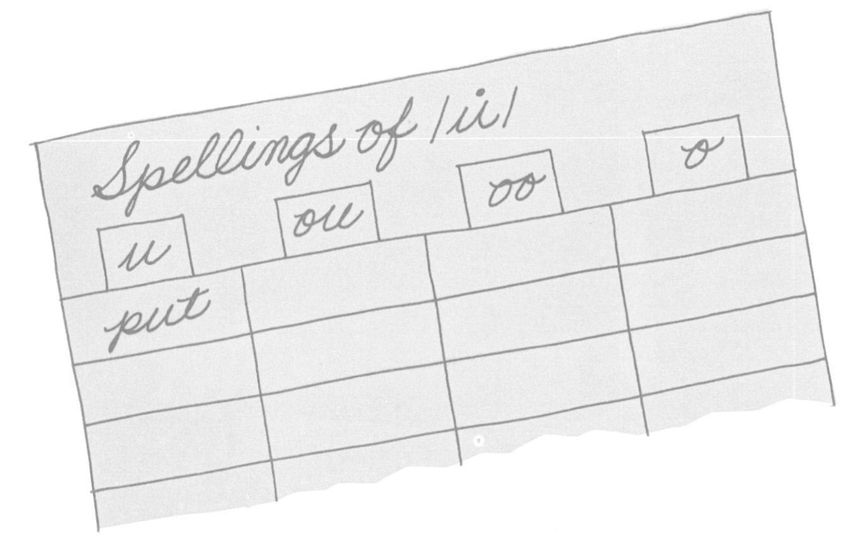

Perhaps you can think of other words that have this sound. Use a dictionary or any other book to find more words with /u̇/.

Sudden Wooden Mountains? Certainly!

A Rewrite the following words.
Draw a line between the first
and second syllables in each word.

kitten   curtain   hidden

Look at the pronunciation codes for these words.

/ˈkit-n/   /ˈkərt-n/   /ˈhid-n/

How many syllables does each word have?

Which syllable in each word is accented?

What sound is heard in the unaccented syllables?

When /n/ forms a syllable by itself,
it is called a *syllabic n*.

In the words you wrote,
kitten, curtain, and *hidden,*
circle the vowel and consonant letters
that spell the syllabic *n*.

B Say each of the following words.
Each one has a syllabic *n*.
Write each word
as it should be spelled.
Then check the spellings
in your Spelling Dictionary.

1 /ˈsəd-n/
2 /ˈbət-n/
3 /ˈlis-n/
4 /ˈkät-n/
5 /ˈwu̇d-n/
6 /ˈmau̇nt-n/
7 /ˈsərt-n/
8 /ˈkəz-n/

Fiddle-Faddle!

A Say the following words.
Listen to the last syllable
in each word.

pencil /ˈpen-səl/
camel /ˈkam-əl/
final /ˈfīn-l/
candle /ˈkan-dl/

How many syllables
does each word have?

Which syllable is accented?

What consonant sound do you hear
in the unaccented
syllables of all four words?

At the end of *pencil, camel, final,* and *candle* you hear /l/ or /əl/. Different dictionaries show the sound in different ways. In some dictionaries the pronunciation code for *camel* is /'kam-l/. In other dictionaries the pronunciation code for *camel* is /'kam-əl/. In each of the other words, some dictionaries will show /ə/ before /l/, and other dictionaries won't. How does your Spelling Dictionary show the pronunciation of *camel?*

B Look again at the four words at the beginning of this exercise. What vowel and consonant are used in each word to spell /l/ or /əl/?

C Complete each word below. Write the correct spelling of /l/ or /əl/. Decide if it is **-il, -al, -el,** or **-le.**

1 anim ___	**5** sadd ___	**9** midd ___
2 pup ___	**6** nick ___	**10** ev ___
3 ab ___	**7** troub ___	**11** met ___
4 mod ___	**8** squirr ___	**12** syllab ___

Cinquains

A *cinquain* is a word picture written in five lines. Read the following cinquain and the directions on how it was developed.

Robin	one word — the title
Red breast	two words — the description
Hopping, dancing, flying,	three words — the action
Singer to the spring	four words — your feelings
Bird	one word — another word for the title

Think of something you'd like to write about in a cinquain. Follow the same pattern as the cinquain about the robin.

More consonant clusters 21

A In Unit 16 you worked with consonant clusters, or blends, that begin with *s*. Now look at the words to the right. Each word begins with a consonant cluster.

break crow prune grandma

What letter is in every consonant cluster?

The consonant cluster in each of the following words is underlined. For each consonant cluster, write two more words with the same cluster. Circle the letters that make up the clusters in the words you write.

1 brush	3 draw	5 hungry	7 trap
2 across	4 fresh	6 pretty	

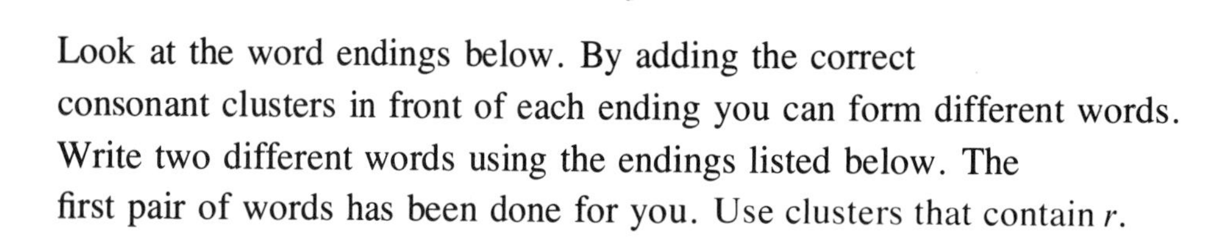

B List seven consonant clusters containing *r*. Use the words in the list in Part A to help you.

Look at the word endings below. By adding the correct consonant clusters in front of each ending you can form different words. Write two different words using the endings listed below. The first pair of words has been done for you. Use clusters that contain *r*.

1 cr op drop	**5** ____ y	**9** ____ ack
2 ____ ove	**6** ____ ow	**10** ____ ave
3 ____ ew	**7** ____ eam	**11** ____ ank
4 ____ ight	**8** ____ eat	**12** ____ own

Verb helpers–have, has, had

A Read the following sentences.

Luis wants to see us beat the Middle City team.
We have beaten the Middle City team once already.

The second sentence is about something that has already happened.

What letters have been added to the verb *beat?*

What verb helper is used with the verb *beaten?*

The helping verbs *have, has,* and *had* can be used with verbs ending with **-en.**

They have eaten here once.
He has eaten here, too.
Bill had eaten there and said the food was good.

To add **-en** to a verb, follow the same spelling patterns used to add **-er** to a word. If you want to review the patterns, turn back to page 55 in Unit 14.

B Use each of the following verbs with the helping verb *have, has,* or *had* in a sentence. Remember to add **-en** to each verb since you are using a helping verb with it.

1 fall	**3** got	**5** broke
2 chose	**4** take	**6** bit

Word builders-prefixes

A Say the following words.

rebuild repay
unhappy unbutton
dishonest disbelieve

Each underlined word part is a *prefix*. Is a prefix added before or after a base word?

Make a chart like the one shown. Each of the words shown on the chart can be used with two or three of the prefixes to form new words. Look at each word and decide what prefixes can be used with it. Then write the new words on the same line with the base word. Be sure to write the words in the correct prefix column. The first one has been done for you.

	re-	un-	dis-
1 do	redo	undo	
2 able			
3 load			
4 fresh			
5 appear			
6 cover			

B What meaning does the prefix **re-** add to a base word?

What meaning does the prefix **un-** add to a base word?

What meaning does the prefix **dis-** add to a base word?

Calendar caper

Listed on the next page are nine holidays in the year and the days when they are celebrated. Only some of the letters have been included. You must supply the missing letters. When you have finished writing the names of the holidays, write all the circled letters in order. Then divide them into words to spell out a secret message. Do you agree with the message?

Wa ___ ___ ___ ngt ___ ___ ' ___   ___ ___ rth ___ ___ ___ ,

○○ ird Monday in F○○ ___ ___ ___ ___ ___ ___

S○ c ___ nd Monday in ___ ___ to ___ ___ ___ ,

Col ___ mb ___ ○ Day

Vete ___ a ___ s Day, fo ___ ___ ___ ○ M○ ___ ___ ay

in ___ ct ___ ___ ___ ___ ___

___ ___ ○ ___ 4th, Ind ___ p ___ n○ en ___ ___ ___ ○y

F○ ___ st M ___ ___ ___ ___ ___ ___ in Septem ___ ___ ___ ,

Lab ___ ___ Day

___ ○○ rth ___ ___ ___ ○ sday in ___ ___ ve ___ ○ ___ ___ ,

___ ___ ___ ___ ___ ___ ___ ___ ___ ○ ___ ing D ___ ___

Mem ___ ○ i ___ ___ Day, 1 ___ ___ ○ Monday in ___ ___ ___

___ ___ cem ___ ___ ___ ___ ___ th, ___ ○ ___ ___ ___ ___ ___ mas Day

New ___ ___ ___ ___ 's ○○○, J ___ ___ ___ ___ ___ ___ ___ 1st

/ȯ/ as in a Tall Ball took a Fall 22

A Say the following words. Listen to the vowel sound in each word.

pause fault fawn wash soft brought

Did you hear /ȯ/ in all of the above words?

Make a chart like the one shown for the different spellings of /ȯ/. Write *pause, fault, fawn, wash, soft,* and *brought* in the correct columns on your chart. Circle the letter or letters that spell /ȯ/.

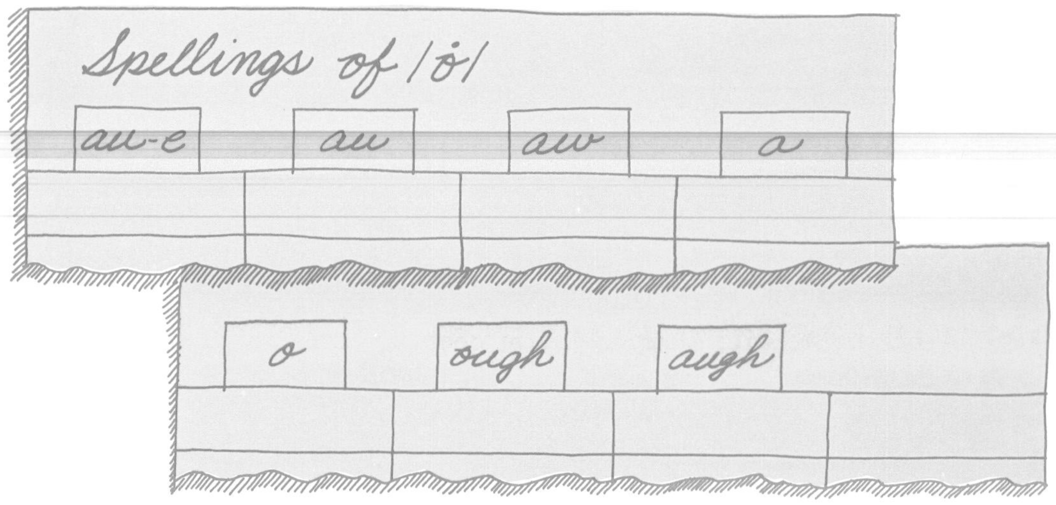

B Say the following words. Listen for /ȯ/.

horn because saw call caught fought

How is /ȯ/ spelled in each word? Write each of the words in the correct column of your chart. Circle the letters that spell /ȯ/.

C Below are pronunciation codes for several words. Write the correct spelling for each word. Check the spellings in your Spelling Dictionary. Then write each word in the correct column of your chart and circle the letters that spell /ȯ/.

1 /shȯrt/ **3** /bȯt/ **5** /wȯl/ **7** /ˈkȯf-ē/

2 /lȯn/ **4** /ˈkȯr-nər/ **6** /kȯz/ **8** /krȯs/

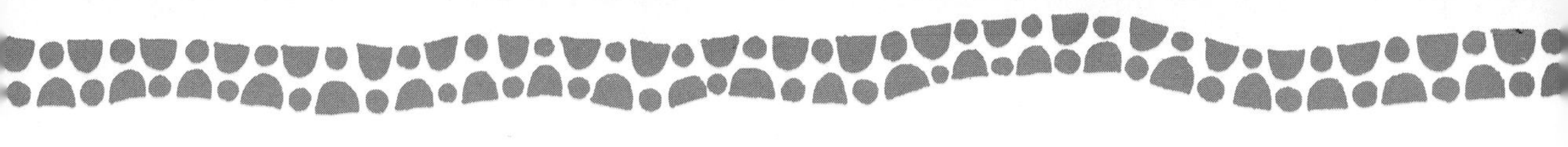

D Some people pronounce some of the following words with /ȯ/, as in *saw*, and some with /ä/, as in *top*.

Say each word. If you pronounce it with /ȯ/, write /ȯ/ for the vowel sound. If you pronounce it with /ä/, write /ä/ for the vowel sound.

1 fog **2** bog **3** wash **4** frog **5** log **6** hog

Abbreviations

A **Extension.** Certain words often are written in a short form. The short form is called an *abbreviation*. Names of the states, titles used with people's names, and measurements are often abbreviated. You can find the meaning of an abbreviation in a dictionary.

Write out the full word that each abbreviation below stands for. Then check the abbreviations in a dictionary.

1 co. **5** mi. **9** Aug.

2 oz. **6** min. **10** hr.

3 qt. **7** yd. **11** in.

4 jr. **8** Dr. **12** Pa.

B Answer the following questions about abbreviations.

1 What punctuation mark usually follows an abbreviation?

2 With what kind of letter do titles used with people's names begin?

3 What title that is not an abbreviation can be used with an unmarried woman's name?

4 Have you ever seen or used the title *Ms.?* Is this title used with a married woman's name, an unmarried woman's name, or can it be used with both?

C Write the name and title, such as *Mr., Ms., Mrs., Miss, Dr.,* for the following people.

1 your teacher **3** your father
2 your mother **4** your doctor

Guide words

A *Guide words* in a dictionary are the two words at the top of each page. Guide words help you find a word in the dictionary more easily. The guide word at the top-left side of each page is the first word defined on that page. The guide word at the top-right side of each page is the last word defined on that page. Look at the following example from a dictionary.

hotel 150 **humbug**

ho·tel /hō-ˈtel/ *n.* a place that supplies rooms and food to travelers and others.

hour /au̇r/ *n.* **1.** sixty minutes of time. **2.** the time of day. **3.** the time for anything: *The lunch hour begins at 11:30.*

huge /hyüj/ *adj.* very large; unusually big.

hum·bug /ˈhəm-bəg/ *n.* a cheat. *v.* to cheat; to deceive with a sham.

1 What are the guide words for the page shown?
2 What is the first word defined on the page?
3 What is the last word defined on the page?

B Look at the words below. Write p. 150 for each word that would come on the same page as the guide words **hotel** and **humbug**. Write B for each word that would come before that page. Write A for each word that would come after that page.

1 howl
2 human
3 house
4 hut
5 hot
6 hook
7 how
8 hug
9 humdinger
10 hull
11 huff
12 hunger
13 hunch
14 hubbub

Borrowed words

A Languages change in many ways. One way is by adding words from other languages. Many words have come into the English language of the United States from the Spanish language of Mexico.

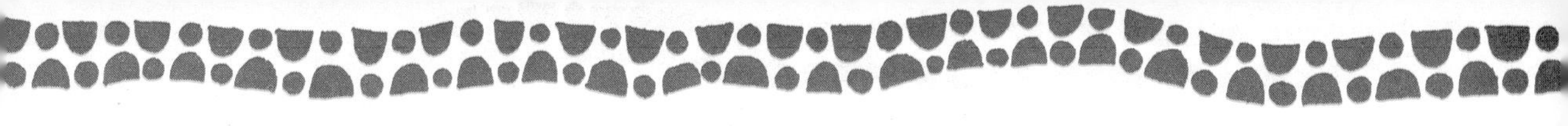

Some words have come into English from Spanish without any changes at all, such as *coyote*. Other words that have come into use in English from Spanish have changed slightly in spellings, pronunciations, and meanings, such as *vamoose*. The English word *vamoose* is pronounced /və-'müs/. It means "to leave quickly." *Vamoose* developed from the Spanish word *vamos*. *Vamos* is pronounced /'vä-mōs/ and means "let us go."

Look at the following Spanish words and their pronunciations and meanings. Can you be a word detective?
Write the English word that developed from each of these Spanish words.

1 lazo /'läs-ō/ a loop; a lariat

2 rodear /rō-'dā-är/ a going around; a round-up of cattle

3 mosca /'mō-skə/ a fly *and* **-ito** /ē-tō/ little

B Listed below are some Spanish-American names. Write what you think the same name would be in English. The first one has been done for you.

1 Miguel *Michael*	**4** Tomaso	**7** Alícia
2 Alfredo	**5** Roberto	**8** Ana
3 María	**6** Eduardo	

Animals in adventure

Do you know what kinds of animals live in the Southwest? Coyotes, sheep, bulls, horned toads, desert turtles, horses, cattle, snakes, bobcats, kit foxes, and many more kinds of animals live there.

Write a report about an animal that lives in the Southwest. You can find facts about the animal in a book or an encyclopedia.

Commas in a series? Yes, yes, yes!

A Read the sentence at the right.

Mary Jane Betty Lou and Sally came to the party.

Do you know for sure how many different people are named in the sentence? Is there really just one girl named Mary Jane Betty Lou? Mary Jane could be one person or two people. The same is true of Betty Lou. Commas should be used in the right places to separate the names.

Mary Jane, Betty Lou, and Sally came to the party.

or

Mary, Jane, Betty, Lou, and Sally came to the party.

Three or more items listed in a sentence are called a *series*. The girls' names make up a series. If you had spoken the sentence, you probably would have left a very short pause between the names of the different people. A listener would have known how many people you were talking about.

When you are writing a series, you use a comma after each item in the series except the last one. For example, a comma should follow each person's name except *Sally* in the sentences above.

Read the sentences below. Decide how many items are in each series. Rewrite each sentence. Put commas in to separate the items in the series.

1 We took fried chicken potato chips and lemonade to the picnic.

2 Is your favorite sport baseball football basketball or track?

3 Do you have brown blue hazel or green eyes?

4 Lynn had to run skip hop jump and chin herself for the gym test.

B Write a sentence which includes a list of at least three items. Use commas to separate the items in the series.

C Read the sentences at the right and notice where commas are used.

Yes, I'm ready for the big game.
No, I've got to practice some more.

Do you use commas after *yes* and *no* when they come at the beginning of sentences?

D Rewrite each of the following sentences.
Put commas wherever they are needed.

1 Yes I remember meeting you at the fair last year.
2 No we didn't buy any bananas oranges pears or apples.
3 Yes we used all the tables chairs benches and stools we could find.

E Answer each of the following questions with a complete sentence.
Begin your answers to questions 4 and 5 with *yes* or *no*.

1 What are three of your favorite foods?
2 What are three of your favorite TV programs?
3 What four games do you like to play?
4 Do you like to read library books?
5 Do you collect anything?

One or more

A To form a plural word, you usually add **-s** or **-es** to the singular form. Read the following examples.

picnic — picnics   bush — bushes

How do you form the plural of words ending in *f* or *fe*? For some of these words, you just add **-s** to form the plural. Read the following examples.

chief — chiefs   giraffe — giraffes

But other nouns ending with *f* or *fe* form the plural in an irregular way. Look at the following examples.

leaf — leaves   shelf — shelves

1 With what sound do the words *leaf* and *shelf* end?

2 What two sounds do you hear at the end of the plural forms *leaves* and *shelves?*

3 What letters replace the *f* or *fe* to spell /vz/?

B Read the words below. Say the plural form of each word. Decide if the plural ends with /s/ or /vz/. Then write the correct spelling of each plural form.

1 self	**3** roof	**5** wife	**7** knife	**9** belief
2 calf	**4** loaf	**6** wolf	**8** life	**10** half

/kw/ as in the **Quick Queen Quacked**

A Say the following words and listen to the first two sounds you hear in each one.

quart quiz
question quote

What consonant sounds do you hear blending at the beginning of these words?

What two letters spell those sounds?

B Write the correct spelling for each pronunciation code below. Check your answers in your Spelling Dictionary.

1 /kwik/ **3** /kwīt/

2 /kwit/ **4** /ˈkwī-ət/

C Write the correct word, *quick, quiet, quit,* or *quite,* to complete each of the following sentences.

1 Andrew ____ the basketball team.

2 A library is usually a very ____ place.

3 You have to be very ____ to beat Jenny to the drinking fountain.

4 It is ____ hot in the lunchroom today.

Syllables

A Read the following sentence.

> Would you rejoin us
> after you finish your lunch?

How many syllables
does the underlined word have?

The first syllable is a prefix.
When a prefix is added to a base word, the prefix often forms a separate syllable.

Rewrite each word below. Then divide each word into syllables by drawing a circle around the base word.

1 replant	**4** reborn
2 unload	**5** dismount
3 dislike	**6** unpack

B Now rewrite each of the following words. Divide each word into syllables by drawing a circle around the base word.

1 mighty	**6** parted
2 catcher	**7** wooden
3 greatest	**8** careful
4 spelling	**9** rancher
5 rainy	**10** quickly

The second syllable in each word is a suffix. When a suffix is added to a base word, the suffix usually forms a separate syllable.

Which is accented in each of the words in Part B, the base word or the suffix?

C Where is a word usually divided into syllables when it has a prefix or a suffix?

Rewrite each of the following words.
Draw lines to show where you would divide each word into syllables.

1 rereading	**4** dismounting
2 replanted	**5** unhelpful
3 unkindly	**6** untying

/sh/ as in Shouldn't Shorty Share the Sugar? 24

Say the words *sock* and *shock*.

1 With what sound does *sock* begin?

2 What letter spells that sound?

3 With what sound does *shock* begin?

4 What letters spell that sound?

Now say the words *sure* and *sugar*.

5 With what sound do these two words begin?

6 How is that sound spelled in *sure* and *sugar?*

Below are several pronunciation codes. Write the correct spelling for each word. Check the spellings in your Spelling Dictionary.

1 /sheər/	**3** /shu̇r/	**5** /shel/	**7** /shüt/
2 /shü/	**4** /shau̇t/	**6** /ˈshu̇g-ər/	**8** /shȯrt/

Make two columns on a separate sheet of paper. Head one column "/sh/ spelled *sh*" and the other column "/sh/ spelled *s*." Put each of the words in Part B in the correct column on your paper.

Find other words that begin with /sh/. Write them in the correct columns on your paper. You could use a reader, another text, or a dictionary to find more words.

Review of /ə/

Look at the pronunciation codes below. Say each word. Write the correct spelling for each one. Check the spellings in your Spelling Dictionary. Then circle the letters that spell /ə/ in each word.

1 /ˈā-prəl/	**4** /ə-ˈmau̇nt/
2 /ˈwən-dər/	**5** /ˈsev-ən/
3 /ˈsē-krət/	**6** /kləb/

Syllables

A Say the words *saved* and *shared*.

How many vowel sounds do you hear in these words?

How many syllables does each word have?

Say the words *planted* and *seated*.

How many vowel sounds do you hear in these words?

How many syllables does each word have?

B Say each of the following words. Decide if it has one syllable or two syllables. Write the words that have one syllable in a column under *shared*. Write the words that have two syllables in a column under *planted*. Divide the two-syllable words by drawing a line between the syllables.

boarded	socked	pointed	acted
baked	posted	smoked	loaded
raised	sighted	dusted	billed
pounded	smelled	sewed	cared

C Look at the words in the column under *planted*. What consonant letters come just before the suffix **-ed** in these words?

Do these letters come just before the **-ed** in any of the words in the column headed *shared?*

Complete the following pattern based on what you have noticed in the two columns of words you made.

If the suffix **-ed** follows the consonants ____ or ____, **-ed** forms a separate syllable, as in the word ____.

What is the end of everything?

A Rewrite the following compound words. Decide where they should be divided into syllables. Then draw a line to divide each word.

fireplace airplane

What two words make up the first compound word?

What two words make up the second compound?

Compound words are divided into syllables between the whole word parts.

B Read the following compound words and notice how they are divided into syllables.

handyman **hand·y·man**

lifesaving **life·sav·ing**

Are these compound words divided between the whole word parts?

Are they divided into syllables anywhere else?

Rewrite each of the following compound words.
Divide each word into syllables.
First, draw a line between the words that form the compound.
Then draw lines to divide any other syllables.
Use what you have learned about syllables to divide these words.

1 anybody	**4** somebody	**7** Thanksgiving
2 grandmother	**5** nobody	**8** everywhere
3 newspaper	**6** policeman	

After you have finished,
check your work in your Spelling Dictionary.

Haiku

For over three hundred years, the Japanese
have been writing a special form of poem called *haiku* /'hī-kü/.

Ha! the butterfly!
— is following the person
who stole the flowers!

Anonymous

Soft golden flowers
push winter's sleeping away
with blossoms of hope.

Sharon

What season of the year does each haiku seem to be written about?

There's a special pattern to follow when writing a haiku. Count the number of syllables in each line of the first haiku.

	1 2 3 4 5
Line 1	Ha! the but/ter/fly!
	1 2 3 4 5 6 7
Line 2	— is fol/low/ing the per/son
	1 2 3 4 5
Line 3	who stole the flow/ers.

There are five syllables in the first line,
seven syllables in the second line, and five syllables in the third line.

How many syllables are in each line of the second haiku?

A haiku is a thought about nature. Write a haiku of your own.
You can use one of the subjects listed below or think of one yourself.
Be sure the first line has five syllables, the second line has seven syllables, and the third line has five syllables.

a rose	the ocean	a cricket
a sleepy puppy	a raindrop	a bee
ants at work	night noises	a kite
a windy day	a spider spinning a web	clouds

/s/ as in Sally Sells Seashells at the Seashore

25

A Say the following words. Listen to the consonant sound at the beginning of each word. seventh single city circus

What letters spell beginning /s/ in these words?

Now say these words and listen for the final consonant sound. glass circus else bounce

What letters spell final /s/ in these words?

B Make a chart like the one shown for spellings of /s/. Then write the words listed in Part A in the correct columns of your chart. Circle the letter or letters that spell /s/ in each word.

Spellings of /s/

Beginning /s/	
spelled s	spelled c

Final /s/			
spelled ss	spelled s	spelled se	spelled ce

C Listed at right are some pronunciation codes. Write the correct spelling for each one. Check the words in your Spelling Dictionary. Then add each word to the correct column of your chart. Circle the letter or letters that spell the beginning or the final /s/.

1 /ˈrē-ses/
2 /fens/
3 /ˈsərt-n/
4 /chās/
5 /nərs/
6 /kro̊s/
7 /pants/
8 /smīl/
9 /ˈprin-səs/
10 /ˈspesh-əl/

D Find other words to add to your chart. Look in your books, magazines, or a dictionary.

More word shrinkers

A

Read these words.

I'm you've couldn't haven't

What are words
like these called?

B

Practice word shrinking.
Write contractions for the words
listed at right.
Then, use the second word
of each pair of words listed
to write another contraction.
The first one has been done for you.

1 would not *wouldn't shouldn't*

2 I would

3 they have

4 you will

5 you are

6 there is

7 we had

8 she has

Choose your noun

A English is a word-order language. Certain kinds of words fit into a certain order in a sentence.
Write a word for each blank to make a good sentence.

1 A ____ climbed the ____.

2 The ____ flew into a ____.

3 When he saw the ____,
he ran into a ____.

4 A ____ was left on the ____.

5 An ____ walked past an ____.

The words you wrote are called *nouns*.
What three words come just
before the nouns in these sentences?

These words can be called *noun markers*.
Noun markers signal that a noun is going to follow.

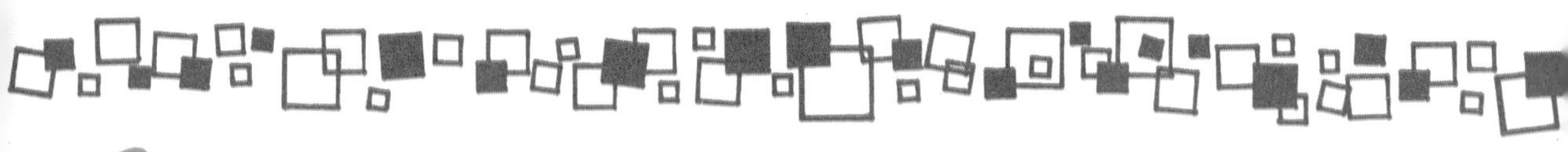

B Rewrite the following story. Write a noun for each blank. You may want to use the same noun more than once.

Once upon a time there was a ____ who liked to sing.
One ____ he met an ____ who liked to work.
This ____ was putting away some ____
for the winter. The ____ wanted the ____
to sing and dance with him, but the ____ kept on working.

Soon it was winter. It became very cold, and there was no more
____ in the land. The ____ was very hungry.
He went to the ____ and said, "Please give me some
____ for I am very hungry." But the ____ said,
"You should have worked in the ____ as I did,
but you wanted to sing instead. Now you can eat your ____."

C In Part B, all of the words you wrote for the blanks should be nouns. Write the answers to the following questions about the nouns you wrote for Part B.

1 Can you add endings like **-ing** or **-ed** to any of the words you wrote?

2 Can you add an **-s** or an **-es** ending to the words? How would these endings change the words?

3 Write the eight noun markers that are used in the story. Write each one only once.

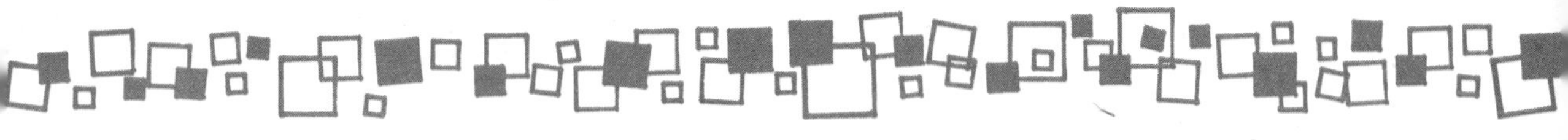

D The following clues can help you decide if a word is a noun. Complete each clue correctly.

Clue 1
A noun is a word that can be ____ so that it means only one or ____ so that it means more than one.

Clue 2
Often, a ____ ____ will signal that a noun is going to follow.

Clue 3
A ____
is any word that will fit into one of the following test sentences.

The ____ is/are nice.

Have you ever seen (a/an) ____?

E Think of six words that can be used as nouns.
Check each word with Clue 1.
Can it be a singular or a plural word?
Check it with Clue 2.
Can it use a noun marker?
Check it with Clue 3.
Does it fit into one of the test sentences in Clue 3?
Write the six nouns you thought of that fit the clues.

Bug's eye view

What would it be like to see things from a bug's eye view?
What would a blade of grass look like?
Would a leaf make a good raft or a roof over your house?
Tell about something seen or done from a bug's eye view.
Write a story about Archie Ant, Lilly Ladybug, Frank Fly, Barny Bug, or any other insect.

/m/ as in the Monster Must Move at Midnight

A Read the following words.
Listen to the beginning consonant
sound of each word.

magic May match
myself mirror

What is the beginning sound of each word?

How is that sound spelled in each word?

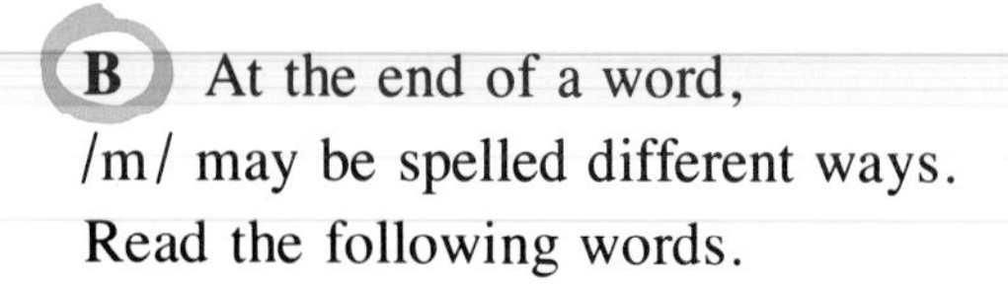

B At the end of a word,
/m/ may be spelled different ways.
Read the following words.

problem calm lamb column

1 How is /m/ spelled in *problem?*
2 How is /m/ spelled in *calm?*
3 How is /m/ spelled in *lamb?*
4 How is /m/ spelled in *column?*

C **Extension.** Write the correct
spelling for each pronunciation code below.
Check your spelling in a dictionary.
Then circle the letter or letters
that spell /m/ in each word.

1 /klīm/	**5** /päm/	**9** /math/
2 /ˈbät-əm/	**6** /mīnd/	**10** /krəm/
3 /mēl/	**7** /lim/	**11** /ˈpō-əm/
4 /ˈpräb-ləm/	**8** /ˈȯt-əm/	**12** /ˈmid-l/

/n/ as in Now the Knights Know it is Noon

A Read the words
below, and listen
to the beginning sound
in each word.

needle knock

nail knob

What sound
do you hear at the
beginning of each word?

How is that sound
spelled in these words?

B Write three words beginning with /n/ spelled *n,* as in *needle*. Write three words beginning with /n/ spelled *kn,* as in *knock*.

C Write a homophone for each word listed below. Each homophone should have the *kn* spelling of /n/ or the *n* spelling of /n/.

1 no **2** knight **3** knot **4** new

Riddle me, Riddle me, Ree

A Complete the answer to each of these riddles.

1 Why might we be worn out if we add **-ed** to us? It will make us ____.

2 Why does the letter *e* make a hug bigger? It makes it ____.

3 Why is a cub afraid of the letter *e*? It will change him into a ____.

B Say the following words and listen for /yü/.

huge music few beautiful

How is /yü/ spelled in each word? Make a chart like the one shown. Write each of the words in a separate column of your chart. Circle the letter or letters that spell /yü/ in each word. Then write the letters you circled in the box at the top of each column.

C Read the following words. Add them to the correct columns of your chart. Circle the letters that spell /yü/.

use beauty future unicorn
pew cube mule uniform

D Look for other words with /yü/ to add to your chart. You can look in a dictionary, reader, or other text. Add the words you find to the correct columns of your chart and circle the letters that spell /yü/. You may have to add new columns to your chart.

Where's the action?

A Each of the sentence parts below needs some action. Complete each sentence by writing a word that will supply the action.

1 The horses ____.
2 Six dancers ____.
3 Some monkeys ____.
4 The jets ____.
5 Every child ____.

The words you wrote to complete the sentences are being used as *verbs*.

B Sentences sometimes have signals that help you recognize a word that is being used as a verb. Read the sentences again. What kind of word comes just before each verb?

In each of the sentences, a verb follows a noun. You probably use the *Noun-Verb* sentence pattern sometimes when you talk or write. In the N-V (Noun-Verb) pattern, the noun is the subject of the sentence. The verb is the *predicate*. The predicate is "the part of the sentence that tells something about the subject."

Write three sentences
that follow the N-V pattern.

Noun (Subject)	Verb (Predicate)
A lion	roars.

C Any word that can be used as a verb will fit into one of the following test frames. The verb *roars* fits into the first test frame. "The child roars."

Use the test frames to test the verbs you wrote for Part B.

1 The child/children ____.
2 The child/children ____ it.
3 The child/children ____ happy.

D You have learned to recognize noun markers. There are also words that may come before a verb to signal that a verb will follow. These words are called *verb markers*. Read this sentence.

The child has gone.

The word *has* is being used as a helping verb, or a verb marker, in this sentence. But verb markers are words that sometimes can be used by themselves as verbs. Read the next sentence. The word *has* is used as a verb in this sentence.

The child has a book.

In the sentence "The child has gone," *has* is a marker and joins with *gone* to form the verb. Which test frame in Part C does *has gone* fit?

In the sentence "The child has a book," *has* is the verb. Which test frame in Part C does the verb *has* fit?

E Write four sentences. Underline the verb in each of your sentences. Test each verb in the test frames in Part C.

/ȯ/ as in I Caught a Hawk that could Talk

A Which three words in the title have /ȯ/ in them? Write those three words. Circle the letters in each word that spell /ȯ/.

B Each of the following words has /ȯ/. For each word, write two more words that have the same spelling of /ȯ/. Circle the letters that spell /ȯ/.

call	saw	cloth

C Given below are definitions for six words. The word for each definition contains /ȯ/. Write the correct word for each definition. Circle the letters that spell /ȯ/.

1 the eighth month of the year

2 ground around a house or in a park that is covered with grass

3 a dog's foot

4 little in size

5 for the reason that (I can't play yet ____ I'm still eating.)

6 got by paying for

D You have circled seven different spellings of /ȯ/ in the words in this exercise. Write the seven different spellings that you have circled.

Adjectives

A Read through the following story. After you have finished reading it, go back to the beginning. In each space, write a word that tells about the noun that follows the blank. After you have finished, write a title for the story.

Once upon a time there was a/an ____ village called Ticklemee. In a/an ____ house on a/an ____ road in the village, there lived a/an ____ woman named Bea Silly and her ____ pig, Chubs.

One day Bea Silly saw a/an ____ child pass her house. Because the ____ woman wanted Chubs to be a very clean pig, she called out to the child that she would pay five dollars to have her ____ pig given a bath. The ____ child took the job. But, that child learned that not all baths are ____ baths.

B Each word you wrote for the story in Part A should tell something about the noun that follows it. The words that describe the nouns are called *adjectives*.

Look through the story again. What are most of the words that come just before the adjectives called?

What kind of word follows each adjective?

C Usually, a word that can be used as an adjective will fit into one of these test frames.

We are very ____.
It is very ____.

Test each of the words below. For each word that fits one of the test frames, write a sentence using the word as an adjective.

1 beautiful	**4** quit	**7** silly	**10** brainy
2 huge	**5** brain	**8** mirror	**11** smooth
3 being	**6** jumpy	**9** heavy	**12** recess

Consonant clusters

A Say the words below. Listen to /kr/, /tr/, /pr/, and /kw/ in the words. Notice how the two consonant sounds at the beginning of each word blend together. Write two more words for each consonant cluster.

cream trap print quint

B Make new words by adding *s* to the beginning of each word below. Write each new word. Circle the beginning consonant cluster in each word.

1 cream
2 trap
3 quint
4 print
5 train
6 crawl

C Read the following definitions. All of the words that answer the definitions begin with a three-letter consonant cluster and start with *s*. Write the answers. Then circle the beginning consonant cluster in each word you wrote.

1 unusual, unfamiliar
2 a sharp sound like that made by a mouse
3 to write carelessly
4 a light rain
5 a small animal with a bushy tail
6 a small river
7 to rub hard in washing
8 the season between winter and summer

D Write the eight consonant clusters used in Parts A and B. Four of them are two-letter clusters, and four of them are three-letter clusters.

Make a sentence grow

A People don't often use the N-V sentence pattern in its simplest form. Read the following sentences. They are examples of how the simplest N-V sentence can be developed into a more descriptive, interesting sentence.

a The monkey (N) swings (V).

b The small, brown monkey (N) swings (V) through the trees.

c The small, brown monkey (N) with the crooked tail swings (V) happily through the trees.

1 Which noun is the subject of each sentence?
2 What is the verb in the predicate of each sentence?

B Many words can be added to a sentence in the N-V pattern without changing the sentence pattern. Make the following N-V sentences grow by adding words to each sentence.

1 A child laughed.
2 The frog leaped.
3 An elephant came.
4 The sheriff ran.
5 Five sharks swam.
6 Every person jumped.

The Mystery Month

The words listed below are written in a secret code. Each letter stands for the letter that comes just before it in the alphabet. For example, *T* stands for *S*.

Copy the puzzle shown. Decode each word. Write it in the correct place in the puzzle. When you have finished, the letters in the circles will spell the mystery month.

1 T U S B O H F
2 T R V J S S F M
3 I V H F
4 R V J U
5 I J N T F M G
6 N B U D I

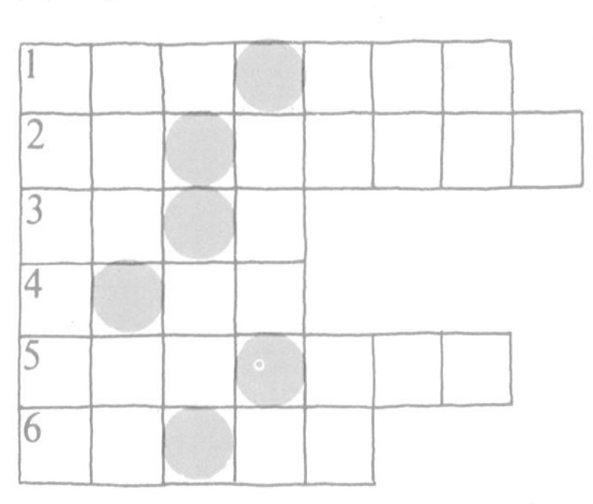

Why is the letter k like a pig's tail?

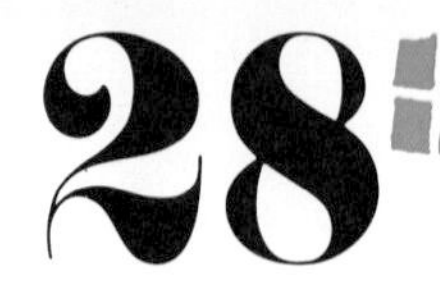

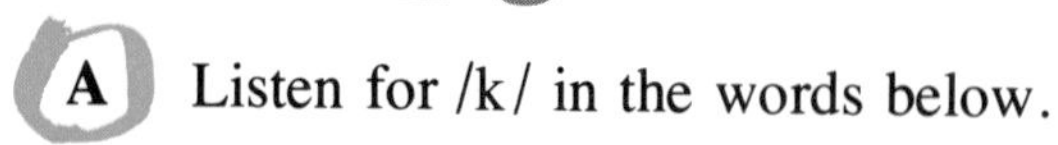

A Listen for /k/ in the words below.

kitchen captain junk music brick

What letters can spell /k/
at the beginning of a word?

What letters can spell /k/
at the end of a word?

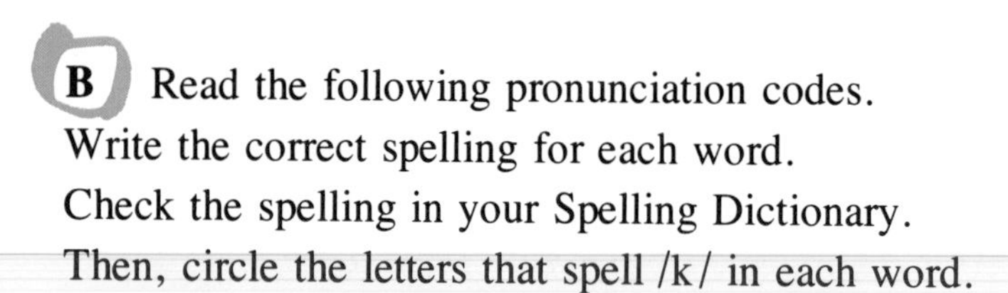

B Read the following pronunciation codes.
Write the correct spelling for each word.
Check the spelling in your Spelling Dictionary.
Then, circle the letters that spell /k/ in each word.

1 /ōk/ **3** /spēk/ **5** /rek/ **7** /silk/ **9** /dark/ **11** /stək/

2 /chik/ **4** /kāv/ **6** /'maj-ik/ **8** /kid/ **10** /'kab-ən/ **12** /kȯz/

C What letters can spell /k/ when it's in the middle of a word?
Write the following words. Then, circle the letter or letters
that spell the middle /k/ in each word you wrote.

1 act **2** pocket **3** escape

4 broken **5** ticket **6** thankful

Little leaves love Level limbs

A **1** What sound do you hear at the beginning of each word in the title?

2 How is that sound spelled?

3 Which two words in the title end with /l/ and /əl/?

B Say the following words.
Listen to the syllabic *l* or /əl/ at the end of each word.

ankle squirrel final April pistol

Make a chart
like the one shown.
Write *ankle, squirrel,*
final, April, and *pistol*
in separate columns
on your chart.
Circle the letters
that spell /l/ or /əl/
in each word.
Then write those letters
in the box above each word.

C Read the following words.
Write each word in the correct column of your chart.
Circle the letters that spell /l/ or /əl/.

metal cattle pupil barrel

D The suffix **-ful** has /əl/. How is /əl/ spelled in this suffix?
Add the suffix **-ful** to each of the following words.
Write the new words on your spelling chart.
Circle the letters that spell /əl/.
You may have to begin a new column.

beauty care wonder thank

E Can you find other words that end in /l/ or /əl/?
Look in a newspaper, a book, or a dictionary.
Write the words you find in the correct columns of your chart.
Circle the letters that spell /l/ or /əl/.

Verb signals

Suffixes can help you to know how a word is being used in a sentence. What suffixes are sometimes used with verbs? Read the sentences at right. Notice the different verb markers and the suffixes used with the verbs.

The child will shout.

The child shouts.

The child is shouting.

The child shouted.

The child has taken a toy.

1 What three helping verbs are used in the sentences?

2 What four suffixes are used with the verbs?

3 Write the five verbs. Don't forget to include the helping verb (the verb marker).

Adverbs—How? When? Where?

A *Adverbs* give how, when, or where information about a verb. Read the sentences at right.

Robin Hood escaped.

Robin Hood escaped quietly.

Robin Hood quietly escaped.

Quietly, Robin Hood escaped.

The sentences give you some clues that help you to recognize adverbs.

1 Which word is the verb in the sentences?

2 Which word tells you how Robin Hood escaped?

3 What suffix has been added to *quiet?*

4 Can adverbs have different positions in sentences?

B Most adverbs will fit into the following test frame.

Victor Jones danced ____.

Test some words in the adverb test frame.
Write six words that can be used as adverbs.
Then, write sentences using the six adverbs.

Another sentence pattern

A Read the following scrambled words.
Write them in a normal sentence pattern.

the smelled flowers Terry.

1 Which word is the subject?

2 Which word is the verb?

3 Which words tell what Terry smelled?

4 Is the word *flowers* being used as a noun, verb, or adjective in the sentence?

The sentence follows a N-V-N (Noun-Verb-Noun) pattern.
In the N-V-N sentence pattern, the noun after the verb is the object of the verb. *Terry* is the subject. *Smelled the flowers* is the predicate.

B Write a noun for each sentence part below to complete the N-V-N sentence pattern. You may want to use noun markers and adjectives, too.

1 Our dog chased _____.

2 Suzie and Charlie fixed _____.

3 The group was singing _____.

4 A few girls were painting _____.

5 Six guys played _____.

Solid and
squat in
its tiny pot, my vine climbed out and around and about.

with words, we can
get to the point
just like this
but, talking in circles
the point
we'll miss

Shape poems

Sometimes it can be fun to make poems in the shape of whatever you're writing about. Read the shape poems at the left and then try to write one yourself. (Remember, poems don't have to rhyme.)

Where does chocolate come from? 29

A Chocolate comes from the seeds of the cacao (/kə-ˈkā-ō/) tree.
The cacao tree grows in a tropical climate. The cacao seeds, or beans,
became known as *cocoa beans* in English-speaking countries.
This was probably due to a mistake in spelling by English importers.

The word *cacao* comes from a Maya Indian word meaning ''bitter juice.''
The word *chocolate* came from a Mayan word meaning ''warm beverage.''

How do you say the word *chocolate?*
Some words can be pronounced in more than one way.
Dictionaries may show two or more different ways to pronounce a word.

B Look at the pronunciation codes at the far right. There are two pronunciations listed for each word. Choose the pronunciation code that represents the way you pronounce each word. Write the complete code. Then, write the correct spelling for each word. Check the spellings in your Spelling Dictionary.

1 /ˈchäk-ə-lət/ or /ˈchȯk-ə-lət/
2 /ˈrē-ˌsəs/ or /ri-ˈsəs/
3 /ˈtō-ərd/ or /tə-ˈwȯrd/
4 /ˌhal-ə-ˈwēn/ or /ˌhäl-ə-ˈwēn/
5 /ˈȯf-ən/ or /ˈȯf-tən/
6 /ˈnüz-ˌpā-pər/ or /ˈnyüz-ˌpā-pər/

Why does the Ocean get angry?

Say the words *shell, sugar, bush,* and *dash.*

1 With what sound do *shell* and *sugar* begin?
2 How is that sound spelled?
3 With what sound do *bush* and *dash* end?
4 How is that sound spelled?

When /sh/ is in the middle of a word, it is spelled in different ways.

1 What letters spell /sh/ in *ocean?*

2 What letters spell /sh/ in *official?*

3 What letters spell /sh/ in *nation?*

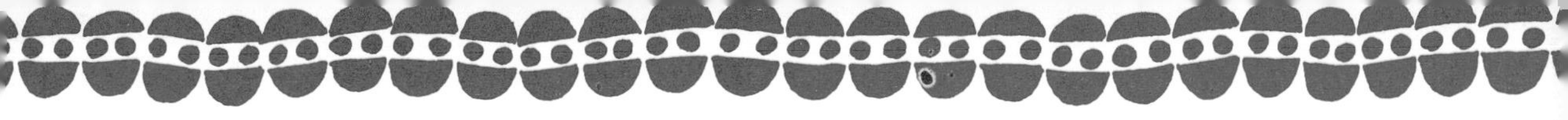

C Read the following pronunciation codes. Write the correct spelling for each word. Check the spellings in your Spelling Dictionary. Then, circle the letters that spell /sh/ in each word.

1 /shärp/	**3** /shu̇r/	**5** /ˈstā-shən/	**7** /ˈspesh-əl/
2 /shōr/	**4** /fresh/	**6** /vā-ˈkā-shən/	**8** /ˈfin-ish/

D **1** What two spellings of the syllable /shən/ can you find in Part B?
2 Which spelling is more common?
3 Find three more words that contain the syllable /shən/. Write those words. Circle the letters that spell /sh/.

Did you find some spellings of /sh/ that are different from the ones in Part A and Part B?

What can you do with Y?

A Say these words. Notice the sound that the circled letter or letters in each word spell.

(y)ou'll	sp(y)	arm(y)	holid(ay)	j(oy)
	b(uy)	hon(ey)	th(ey)	

Make five columns on a piece of paper. Head the columns with /y/, /ī/, /ē/, /ā/, and /ȯi/. Write the title "Sounds Spelled With *y*" on your paper. Then write each of the above words in the correct column on your paper. Circle the letter or letters that spell the sound that the code stands for.

B Read the following words. Add each word to the correct column on your paper. Circle the letter or letters that spell the sound that the code stands for.

yard	you're	young	July	royal	history
probably	destroy	deny	toy	May	hey

C Find other words to add to the columns on your paper. Look in a text, a dictionary, a magazine, or a newspaper.

Reading and writing conversation

A In your reading, you will sometimes find parts where people talk to each other. Read the following examples of a written conversation.

Linda asked, ''What are you doing this afternoon?''

''I was thinking about going swimming,'' said Jenny. ''Do you want to go with me?''

''Hey, that sounds great! Why don't we get some other kids to go, too?'' exclaimed Linda.

''Okay. I'll ask Jerry, Sue, and Laurie. You see if Mary, Joey, and Cindy want to go.''

''I'll tell them to meet us at 2:00. We could ride bikes over to the pool.''

''Good idea. I'll see you about 2:00.''

B Answer the following questions about the conversation you just read.

1 What kind of marks are used to show that words are being spoken?

2 At the end of the exact words of the speaker, does the punctuation mark go outside the quotation marks or inside the quotation marks?

3 In the first line, does the first word Linda spoke begin with a small letter or a capital letter?

4 What is the first punctuation used when Jenny begins speaking the first time?

5 In which paragraph is the question ''Do you want to go with me?''? Who asked that question?

6 How many paragraphs are in the written conversation?

7 You are told who is speaking the first three times but not in the rest of the sentences. You know that Linda doesn't continue speaking. There are clues to signal you each time a different person begins speaking. What are the two signals?

C There are no punctuation marks or capital letters used in the following sentences. Read the sentences. Then, rewrite them using the correct punctuation marks and capital letters.

1 it is so dark in here that i cant see anything carolyn whispered

2 do you think we could go to the park soon begged tim

3 we probably wont be able to finish this tonight said sandy

4 i can see the parade coming down the street exclaimed dick

5 can we buy some potato chips and popcorn at the store asked greg

6 mr moore asked where would you like to go during the summer

7 karen screamed at her dog get out of the street before you get hit

8 you look so silly in the clown suit laughed amy
where are you going dressed like that

9 i wish theyd leave my gate closed growled mr crabbit

10 martha giggled i hope the party will be a real surprise for them

Dash off a dialogue

Tom Sawyer

Eve Merriam

Robin Hood

Queen Elizabeth

Detective Dickens

Rocky Stonewall

The word *dialogue* means ''a conversation between two or more people.'' A dialogue can be written or spoken. Story writers often write dialogue for the people in their stories.

Write a dialogue between two or more people. You can make your dialogue very funny, quite serious, terribly angry, or any mood at all. It might be fun for you to make yourself one of the people in the dialogue. You can choose from some of the names listed, names of your friends, or make up your own characters.

Syllable division 30

A Listed below are some words with the VCCV pattern. Rewrite each word and draw lines between the syllables.

1 rather **2** problem

3 program **4** silver

5 rubber **6** escape

7 either **8** happen

9 September **10** hurry

B Listed below are some words with the VCV pattern. Rewrite each word and draw lines between the syllables.

1 wagon **2** hotel **3** forest

4 police **5** become **6** cabin

7 famous **8** chocolate

9 decide **10** potato

C Listed below are some compound words. Rewrite each word and draw lines between the syllables.

1 airplane **2** airport **3** anyway

4 baseball **5** bedroom **6** daylight **7** everywhere

8 fireplace **9** grandmother **10** policeman

D Listed below are some words with prefixes and suffixes. Rewrite each word and draw lines between the syllables.

1 taken **2** unlock **3** remake

4 farmer **5** during

6 displace **7** thankful **8** removed

9 mostly **10** lasted

11 unshaped **12** reminder

Adding -ed

How would you write the past form of each of the following words? Make a chart like the one shown. Then, write the past form of each word in the correct column of your chart.

whistle	age	bake	invite	expect	ready	apply
fry	plan	chop	slip	reply	care	deny
plant	destroy	board	trap	seem	step	circle
beg	hurry	study	trade	drop	enjoy	block

hop-hopped	*chase-chased*	*try-tried*	*play-played*

Commas in a series

The following sentences have no commas in them. Read the sentences. Then, rewrite each sentence adding commas where they are needed.

1 Please put the salt pepper bread and butter on the table.
2 Did you see the deer goats and other animals at the zoo?
3 Pete had an orange some turkey and a glass of milk for lunch.
4 Stacy likes swimming softball and roller skating in the summer.
5 Make your bed do the dishes and hang up your clothes before you go to the park.
6 Carol Jeff Rose and Teresa are coming to my house after school.
7 It was so hot that I took off my shoes socks and jacket.
8 Nick borrowed a piece of paper a pencil and an eraser.
9 Buy some shampoo toothpaste ice cream and milk at the store.
10 We need some paint chalk string and scissors for this project.

Homophones

The following sentences have wrong homophones in them.
Read the sentences. Then rewrite them using the correct homophones.

1 My ant bought me a blew jump rope today.
2 We read a little about the polar bares that live in the Arctic.
3 The hole sky looks very blew today, don't you think?
4 The movie was over at two o'clock, sew I went home.
5 Hour sun went to a bike sail at a bike store downtown.
6 Which of these too rodes goes to Clayville?
7 Is this the write pear of shoes to wear to the game?
8 "Theirs the circus!" screamed the kids.
9 Your going to go with us, aren't you?
10 The white-tailed dear ran threw the bushes to escape the wolf.

What is it?

A In each of the following sentences, a word is underlined.
Read each sentence. Then write what each word is, a noun, a verb, an adjective, or an adverb.

1 What a beautiful flower garden this is!
2 He nearly lost his balance and fell from the tree.
3 Will you bake some cookies for the club meeting?
4 Sally rolled the huge barrel down the hill.
5 The dog bravely swam to the boy's rescue.
6 Pass the butter to me, please.
7 Who is the captain of the softball team this year?
8 It was a brave act that saved the boy from drowning.
9 I saw your mother and father
sitting on the porch last night at ten o'clock.
10 Decide if it's warm enough to go on a picnic.
11 Use the blue paint to finish this part of your picture.
12 The fireman climbed up the ladder very quickly.

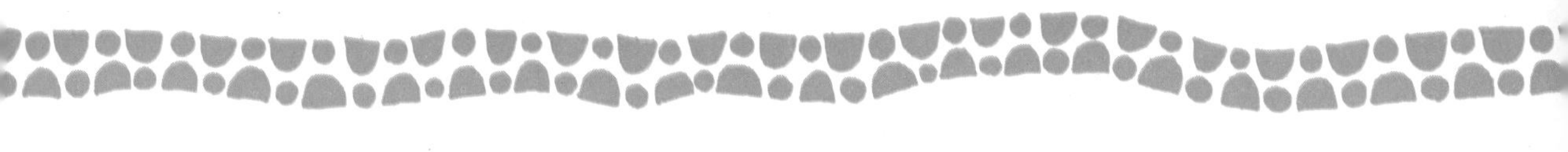

B Listed below in four separate columns are nouns, verbs, adjectives, and adverbs. Write sentences using the words in the noun column as nouns. Do the same for the words in the verb column, the adjective column, and the adverb column.

nouns	**verbs**	**adjectives**	**adverbs**
arrow	chop	dirty	down
bottle	flew	sunny	noisily
cave	raise	orange	quietly

If you need to review nouns, verbs, adjectives, or adverbs, look back to the units where these were presented.
(Nouns—Unit 25, Verbs—Unit 26, Adjectives—Unit 27, Adverbs—Unit 28)

Summer thoughts

What do you do in the summer? Do you belong to a softball team? Do you go swimming a lot? Would you like to visit a faraway place?

Read the following poem. It tells you what Luanne Clifton did during part of a summer day.

Lying on the Grass

You're on your back just thinking
How big the world is and how
Small you are.
All of a sudden you hear something.
It's a robin.
You're lying on the grass and you feel so very good.

Luanne Clifton, Grade 4
Buffalo Grove Schools, Illinois

Write a poem or a story telling what your plans are for the summer. Or write about some great adventure you would like to have or some faraway place you would like to visit during the summer.

Spelling Dictionary

Here is a Pronunciation Key to help you pronounce many of the words in this book. Beside each pronunciation code is a key word with that sound. A short pronunciation key can be found at the bottom of every other page in your Spelling Dictionary.

Pronunciation Key

/a/	bat	/g/	goat	/ng/	ring	/t͟h/	they
/ā/	ape	/h/	horse	/ō/	boat	/u̇/	foot
/ä/	top	/hw/	white	/ȯ/	saw	/ü/	moon
/au̇/	owl	/i/	pin	/ȯi/	oil	/v/	vase
/b/	bear	/ī/	kite	/p/	pipe	/w/	web
/ch/	chair	/j/	jet	/r/	rope	/y/	yarn
/d/	duck	/k/	key	/s/	sun	/z/	zoo
/e/	elf	/l/	leaf	/sh/	sheep	/zh/	treasure
/ē/	eel	/m/	mask	/t/	tooth	/ə/	cup
/f/	fox	/n/	nut	/th/	thing	/ər/	bird

Here is what an entry will look like in this Spelling Dictionary.

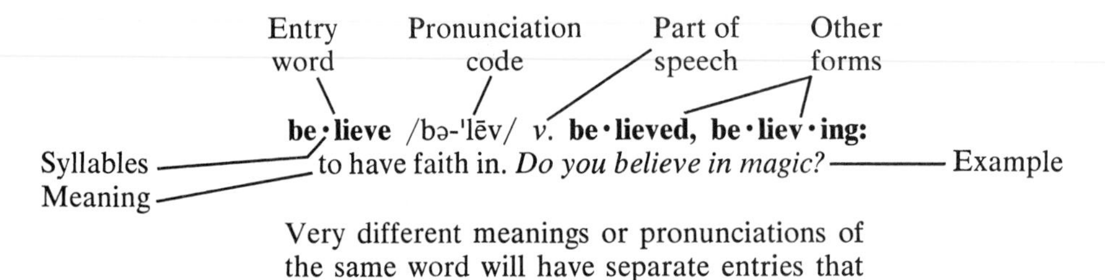

Very different meanings or pronunciations of the same word will have separate entries that are numbered.

List of abbreviations used in this dictionary

n.	= noun	*adv.*	= adverb
pron.	= pronoun	*poss.*	= possessive
v.	= verb	*prep.*	= preposition
adj.	= adjective	*pl.*	= plural

A

a·ble /ˈā-bəl/ *adj.* **a·bler** /ˈā-blər/, **a·blest** /ˈā-bləst/: having the power or skill that is needed.

act /akt/ *n.* thing done; deed: *Caring for animals is an act of kindness. v.* **act·ed, act·ing** 1. to do something: *Jon acted quickly to save the dog.* 2. to play the part of: *Lisa will act the part of Maid Marian in the play.*

age /āj/ *n.* length of life: *Grandpa never told his age. v.* **aged** /ājd/, **ag·ing** or **age·ing:** to grow old: *My aunt seemed to age slowly.*

a·gent /ˈā-jənt/ *n.* person or company who acts for another: *The singer's agent spoke for him.*

a·head /ə-ˈhed/ *adj.* in or toward the front: *Juan is ahead of me in line. adv.* forward: *Go ahead and save seats for us.*

air·plane /'aər-ˌplān/ *n.* winged machine that flies and is driven by a propeller or jet engine.
air·port /'aər-ˌpōrt/ *n.* place for airplanes to land at and start from.
a·like /ə-'līk/ *adj.* much the same or similar: *The cars are very much alike.* *adv.* in the same way: *Karen and Sharon dress alike.*
a·live /ə-'līv/ *adj.* living; not dead.
a·lone /ə-'lōn/ *adj.* or *adv.* apart from other persons or things.
al·read·y /ȯl-'red-ē/ *adv.* before this time; by this time: *He has already gone home.*
A·mer·i·ca /ə-'mer-ə-kə/ *n.* 1. United States. 2. North America and South America.
a·mount /ə-'maůnt/ *n.* sum; total: *The amount of money I had was not enough to buy the toy.* *v.* **a·mount·ed, a·mount·ing:** to reach; to be equal: *The bill amounted to fifteen dollars.*
an·gel /'ān-jəl/ *n.* messenger from God: *The angel told the shepherds that Christ was born.* 2. good and lovely person: *He was an angel while his grandmother was visiting.*
an·kle /'ang-kəl/ *n.* joint connecting the foot with the leg.
an·swer /'an-sər/ *n.* a reply. *v.* **an·swered, an·swer·ing:** to give a reply.
ant /ant/ *n.* small insect that lives in colonies in the ground or in wood.
an·y·bod·y /'en-ē-ˌbäd-ē/ *pron.* any person.
an·y·way /'en-ē-ˌwā/ *adv.* 1. in any event: *If Rick doesn't come, I'll be there anyway.* 2. in any manner: *He tosses his clothes just anyway.*
A·pril /'ā-prəl/ *n.* fourth month of the year.
aren't /ärnt/ are not.
ar·my /'är-mē/ *n. pl.* **ar·mies** 1. large group of soldiers. 2. large group of people working together: *We had an army of helpers.*
ar·row /'ar-ō/ *n.* long, thin stick that is shot from a bow.
a·sleep /ə-'slēp/ *adj.* or *adv.* 1. sleeping. 2. without feeling: *My foot is asleep.*
at·tack /ə-'tak/ *n.* the act of attacking: *Their attack failed.* *v.* **at·tacked, at·tack·ing:** to jump upon or use force against: *The dog attacked the rabbit.*
Au·gust /'ȯ-gəst/ *n.* eighth month of the year.
a·wake /ə-'wāk/ *v.* **a·woke** /ə-'wōk/ or **a·waked, a·wak·ing:** to wake up.
a·while /ə-'hwīl/ *adv.* for a short time: *We waited for awhile.*

B

bake /bāk/ *v.* **baked, bak·ing:** to cook with dry heat as in an oven.
bare /baər/ *adj.* not clothed; uncovered.
bar·rel /'bar-əl/ *n.* 1. container with round, flat top and bottom and curved sides. 2. the metal tube of a gun.
base /bās/ *n.* 1. the part of an object on which it rests; the bottom. 2. station or goal in certain games: *He ran to first base.* 3. headquarters: *There is an Air Force base in town.* *v.* **based, bas·ing:** to set up a foundation for: *Our friendship is based on trust.*
base·ball /'bās-ˌbȯl/ *n.* 1. game played with bat and ball by two teams on a field with four bases. 2. ball used in the game of baseball.
be /bē/ *v.* **was** /wəz/ or /wäz/, **were** /wər/, **been** /bin/, **be·ing, am** /əm/ or /am/, **are** /ər/ or /är/, **is** /iz/ 1. the same in meaning: *You are my friend.* 2. to have a certain quality: *The day was sunny.* 3. to exist; to live. 4. helping verb: *is going.*
beach /bēch/ *n.* sandy shore of a lake or sea. *v.* **beached, beach·ing:** to bring ashore: *The sailor beached his boat.*
bean /bēn/ *n.* 1. smooth seed that grows in a pod. 2. any food shaped like a bean: *We have jelly beans on Easter.*
beat /bēt/ *n.* rhythm or repeated sound in music: *Listen to the beat of the drums.* *v.* **beat, beat·en** /'bēt-n/ or **beat, beat·ing** 1. to hit again and again. 2. to win over someone: *Jenny beat me to the door.* 3. to mix: *Beat the cake batter.*
beau·ti·ful /'byüt-i-fəl/ *adj.* pleasing to see or hear; lovely.
be·come /bi-'kəm/ *v.* **be·came** /bi-'kām/, **become, be·com·ing:** to come to be; to grow to be.
bed·room /'bed-ˌrüm/ or /'bed-ˌrům/ *n.* room to sleep in.
beg /beg/ *v.* **begged, beg·ging** 1. to ask for something free: *On Halloween we beg for treats.* 2. to plead: *Tina begged her mom for a new bike.*
be·ing /'bē-ing/ *n.* living creature: *We are human beings.* *v. form of* BE.
be·lieve /bə-'lēv/ *v.* **be·lieved, be·liev·ing:** to have faith in: *Do you believe in magic?*
be·long /bə-'lȯng/ *v.* **be·longed, be·long·ing** 1. to be owned by. 2. to be a part of or be a member of: *Who can belong to your club?*

belt /belt/ *n.* 1. strip of material worn around the waist. 2. area suited to certain products: *the corn belt.*
be • side /bi-'sīd/ *prep.* at the side of.
be • tween /bi-'twēn/ *prep.* 1. in the space that separates two things: *Don't eat between meals.* 2. by the action of: *Between them they were able to pick two quarts of berries before it rained.*
Bi • ble /'bī-bəl/ *n.* 1. the book of holy writings of the Christian religion. 2. a book of sacred writings of a religion.
bike /bīk/ *n.* bicycle. *v.* **biked, bik • ing:** to ride a bicycle.
[1]**bill** /bil/ *n.* 1. notice of money due for work done or goods given. 2. notice or poster. *v.* **billed, bill • ing:** to send a bill.
[2]**bill** /bil/ *n.* mouth of a bird; beak.
bite /bīt/ *n.* 1. piece of something bitten off. 2. injury made by biting. *v.* **bit** /bit/, **bit • ten** /'bit-n/, **bit • ing** /bīt-ing/: to grab or cut into with the teeth.
blew /blü/ *v. past form of* BLOW.
block /bläk/ *n.* 1. an object of wood, concrete, etc. usually having six sides. 2. space in a town surrounded by streets. *v.* **blocked, block • ing:** to stand or put something in the way of: *The huge dog blocked the doorway.*
bloom /blüm/ *n.* flower. *v.* **bloomed, bloom • ing:** to blossom or produce flowers.
blow /blō/ *n.* a hard hit or stroke. *v.* **blew** /blü/, **blown** /blōn/, **blow • ing** 1. to move swiftly or with power: *a wind blowing.* 2. to send forth a strong current of air: *Blow out the candle.* 3. to make or to cause a sound by blowing: *The trumpets blew loudly.*
board /bōrd/ *n.* 1. thin, long piece of wood. 2. persons who manage or direct an organization: *the school board.* 3. meals provided regularly for a price: *I want to rent a room which includes board.* *v.* **board • ed, board • ing** 1. to go aboard. 2. to provide or get meals for a price. 3. to cover with boards: *We watched as the men boarded up the entrance to the old house.*
bot • tle /'bät-l/ *n.* container with a narrow neck and no handles. *v.* **bot • tled, bot • tling:** to put into a bottle.
bot • tom /'bät-əm/ *n.* lowest part.
bought /bȯt/ *v. past form of* BUY.
[1]**bow** /baů/ *n.* the act of bending: *The queen acknowledged his bow.* *v.* **bowed, bow • ing:** to bend the head or body: *The people bowed to the king.*
[2]**bow** /bō/ *n.* 1. weapon used for shooting arrows. 2. slender rod with horsehairs stretched on it for playing the violin. 3. loops made of string or ribbon.
bowl /bōl/ *n.* 1. hollow rounded dish. 2. bowl-shaped part of anything: *the bowl of a pipe.*
brain /brān/ *n.* mass of nerve cells enclosed in the skull.
branch /branch/ *n.* 1. part of a tree that grows out from the trunk. 2. any offshoot of the main part: *a branch of the main library.* *v.* **branched, branch • ing:** to spread into branches.
brave /brāv/ *adj.* **brav • er, brav • est:** without fear; having courage.
break /brāk/ *n.* the act of breaking: *make a break for safety.* *v.* **broke** /brōk/, **bro • ken** /'brō-kən/, **break • ing** 1. to cause to come apart or to pieces; to destroy or to ruin. 2. to go against: *Do not break any rules.*
break • fast /'brek-fəst/ *n.* first meal of the day.
brick /brik/ *n.* block of clay used in building.
bright /brīt/ *adj.* 1. giving much light. 2. brilliant; rich: *a bright orange color.*
bro • ken /'brō-kən/ *v. form of* BREAK.
broth • er /'brəth-ər/ *n. pl.* **broth • ers** or **breth • ren** /'breth-rən/, *poss.* **broth • er's** 1. man or boy related to someone by having the same parents. 2. person belonging to a certain club or group.
brush /brəsh/ *n.* an object made of bristles attached to a handle and used for cleaning, painting, etc. *v.* **brushed, brush • ing:** to use a brush.
bub • ble /'bəb-əl/ *n.* round coating of liquid surrounding air or gas. *v.* **bub • bled, bub • bling:** to have small, round bodies of air rise to the surface.
build /bild/ *v.* **built** /bilt/, **build • ing:** to put together parts or materials to make something.
bul • let /'bul-ət/ *n.* shaped piece of metal used to shoot from a gun.
bunch /bənch/ *n.* a number of things gathered or growing together. *v.* **bunched, bunch • ing:** to put or to gather together in a bunch.

/a/ bat, /ā/ ape, /ä/ top, /aů/ owl, /e/ elf, /ē/ eel, /i/ pin, /ī/ kite, /ō/ boat, /ȯ/ saw, /ȯi/ oil, /ů/ foot, /ü/ moon, /ch/ chair, /hw/ white, /ng/ ring, /sh/ sheep, /th/ thing, /th/ they, /zh/ treasure, /ə/ cup, /ər/ bird

bush /bůsh/ *n.* small plant with many low branches.

busi • ness /'biz-nəs/ *n.* 1. work that one does; trade: *A policeman's business is to keep order.* 2. company or industry of any kind: *a dry cleaning business.*

bus • y /'biz-ē/ *v.* **bus • ied, bus • y • ing:** to keep moving or active; to work. *adj.* **bus • i • er, bus • i • est:** doing something; active; working.

but • ter /'bət-ər/ *n.* a yellowish fat made by churning cream or milk. *v.* **but • tered, but • ter • ing:** to spread butter on something.

but • ton /'bət-n/ *n.* small object, usually round, used for fastening clothing. *v.* **but • toned, but • ton • ing:** to fasten with a button.

buy /bī/ *n.* something paid for: *This car was a good buy.* *v.* **bought** /bòt/, **buy • ing:** to pay for.

C

cab /kab/ *n.* 1. taxicab. 2. enclosed part of a truck or train where the driver sits.

cab • in /'kab-ən/ *n.* 1. crudely or roughly built one-story house. 2. place for passengers or crew in an airplane or boat.

cab • i • net /'kab-ə-nət/ *n.* 1. piece of furniture used for storing things: *a file cabinet.* 2. group of advisers: *the President's cabinet.*

can • dle /'kan-dl/ *n.* wax with a wick in it to be lighted.

cap • tain /'kap-tən/ *n.* 1. leader or commander. 2. officer.

care /keər/ *n.* attention or interest: *Take care not to break the vase.* *v.* **cared, car • ing:** to feel interest or concern.

care • ful /'keər-fəl/ *adj.* watchful; not reckless.

[1]**case** /kās/ *n.* condition; fact or event: *a case of fire.*

[2]**case** /kās/ *n.* cover or container: *a key case.*

cast /kast/ *n.* actors and actresses in a play. *v.* **cast, cast • ing:** to throw or to toss: *Cast your line in the water.*

cas • tle /'kas-əl/ *n.* large building with thick, high walls and towers; palace with protection against attacks.

catch • er /'kach-ər/ *n.* person or thing that receives something that is thrown.

cat • tle /'kat-l/ *n.* cows, steers, and bulls.

cause /kȯz/ *n.* reason something happens: *What was the cause of the fire?* *v.* **caused, caus • ing:** to be the reason of: *What caused the girl to fall?*

cave /kāv/ *n.* hollow space underground with an opening at the surface. *v.* **caved, cav • ing:** to fall in: *The walls of the building caved in.*

cer • tain /'sərt-n/ *adj.* sure; positive.

chase /chās/ *n.* the act of running after: *The chase tired me.* *v.* **chased, chas • ing** 1. to drive away. 2. to follow in order to catch.

cheese /chēz/ *n.* a food made from milk.

chew /chü/ *v.* **chewed, chew • ing:** to crush or grind with the teeth.

chick /chik/ *n.* young chicken.

choc • o • late /'chäk-ə-lət/ or /'chȯk-ə-lət/ *n.* 1. food made from cacao beans. 2. milk, candy, or other food in which chocolate is used.

chop /chäp/ *n.* slice of meat: *pork chops.* *v.* **chopped, chop • ping** 1. to cut by repeated blows. 2. to cut into small pieces: *Pam chopped carrots for the salad.*

cir • cle /'sər-kəl/ *n.* 1. round drawing: *There's a circle around the correct answer.* 2. ring: *Form a circle around me.* *v.* **cir • cled, cir • cling:** to move round and round: *The plane circled the airport.*

cir • cus /'sər-kəs/ *n.* traveling show with performances by clowns, horses and riders, elephants, and other animals.

climb /klīm/ *v.* **climbed, climb • ing:** to go up or down using the hands and feet.

cloth /klȯth/ *n. pl.* **cloths** /klȯt͟hz/ or /klȯths/: material or fabric.

cloth • ing /'klō-t͟hing/ *n.* coverings for the body; clothes.

club /kləb/ *n.* 1. heavy wooden weapon. 2. people joined together for a purpose. *v.* **clubbed, club • bing:** to hit with a club.

coal /kōl/ *n.* black mineral used for fuel.

cof • fee /'kȯf-ē/ *n.* dark brown drink made from seeds of a tropical plant.

coin /kȯin/ *n.* piece of metal used as money. *v.* **coined, coin • ing:** to make metal money.

com • pa • ny /'kəm-pə-nē/ *n.* 1. a business. 2. guests or visitors.

cool /kül/ *v.* **cooled, cool • ing:** to make or to become cool. *adj.* 1. a little cold. 2. not excited or disturbed; calm.

cor • ner /'kȯr-nər/ *n.* 1. point at which two or more surfaces meet. 2. where two streets meet: *a street corner.* *v.* **cor • nered, cor • ner • ing:** to trap: *The hunters cornered the fox.*

cost /kȯst/ *n.* price of something: *The cost of the ball was too high.* *v.* **cost, cost • ing:** to have the price of: *It cost three dollars.*

cot • tage /'kät-ij/ *n.* small house usually used during vacation.

cot • ton /'kät-n/ *n.* 1. cloth made from the soft, white fibers of the cotton plant. 2. the plant itself. *adj.* made of cotton: *cotton sheets.*

could • n't /'kůd-nt/ could not.

cous • in /'kəz-n/ *n.* son or daughter of one's uncle or aunt.

cov • er /'kəv-ər/ *n.* anything that protects, shelters or hides: *We came ashore under cover of darkness. v.* **cov • ered, cov • er • ing:** to put something on or over in order to protect, shelter or hide: *Mom covered the frying pan.*

crash /krash/ *n.* 1. the noise of things breaking. 2. wreck. *v.* **crashed, crash • ing:** to strike one thing against another: *The car crashed into the tree.*

crew /krü/ *n.* group of people working together, especially on a boat or ship.

cross /krȯs/ *n.* straight stick or post with another across it. *v.* **crossed, cross • ing** 1. to draw a line across: *Cross out your name.* 2. to go from one side to another: *Josh crossed the street.* 3. to place one over the other: *Cross your fingers for luck.*

crown /kraůn/ *n.* 1. headpiece for a king or a queen. 2. top of the head. *v.* **crowned, crown • ing:** to put a crown or a top on: *Greg crowned the pie with whipped cream.*

D

dad /dad/ *n. poss.* **dad's:** father.

date /dāt/ *n.* 1. time; day, month, or year: *What is the date today?* 2. appointment: *Let's make a date for lunch. v.* **dat • ed, dat • ing:** to mark the time on something: *Please date your papers.*

day • light /'dā-ˌlīt/ *n.* the light of day.

dead /ded/ *adj.* 1. without life. 2. dull; not active: *a dead battery.* 3. sure; exact: *a dead shot.*

death /deth/ *n.* end of life.

De • cem • ber /di-'sem-bər/ *n.* twelfth month of the year.

de • cide /di-'sīd/ *v.* **de • cid • ed, de • cid • ing:** to settle; to make a judgment.

deer /diər/ *n. pl.* **deer:** graceful, hoofed animal, the male having antlers.

[1]des • ert /'dez-ərt/ *n.* dry, sandy land with little rainfall and where only a few kinds of plants grow.

[2]de • sert /di-'zərt/ *v.* **de • sert • ed, de • sert • ing:** to leave a person or a thing, especially when one should stay: *The dog has been deserted.*

di • a • mond /'dī-ə-mənd/ *n.* 1. valuable stone, hard and clear, usually used in jewelry. 2. four-sided, pointed shape ◊. 3. baseball infield.

die /dī/ *v.* **died, dy • ing** 1. to stop living. 2. to come to an end little by little: *The storm finally died.*

dif • fer • ent /'dif-ə-rənt/ *adj.* not the same.

dig /dig/ *v.* **dug** /dəg/, **dig • ging:** to turn over dirt or make a hole in the ground.

dirt • y /'dərt-ē/ *adj.* **dirt • i • er, dirt • i • est:** not clean.

dive /dīv/ *n.* the act of diving: *The airplane went into a dive. v.* **dived** or **dove** /dōv/, **div • ing** 1. to plunge downward, headfirst. 2. to plunge or to push forth into anything: *She always dives in and gets her work done quickly.*

doc • tor /'däk-tər/ *n.* person who knows how to treat diseases and illnesses.

drank /drangk/ *v. past form of* DRINK.

draw /drȯ/ *v.* **drew** /drü/, **drawn** /drȯn/, **draw • ing** 1. to pull or haul: *The horses will draw the sleigh.* 2. to make a picture with pen, pencil, paint or the like.

drew /drü/ *v. past form of* DRAW.

drink /dringk/ *n.* a liquid that is swallowed. *v.* **drank** /drangk/, **drunk** /drəngk/, **drink • ing:** to swallow a liquid.

drive /drīv/ *n.* 1. a ride in a car. 2. special effort: *We had a drive to collect old clothing. v.* **drove** /drōv/, **driv • en** /'driv-ən/, **driv • ing** /drī-ving/ 1. to make go: *Drive the pig out of the garden.* 2. to make go where one wants: *I can drive a truck.*

driv • er /'drī-vər/*n.* one who drives.

drove /drōv/ *v. past form of* DRIVE.

dry /drī/ *v.* **dried, dry • ing:** to make or become dry: *Please dry the dishes. adj.* **dri • er, dri • est:** free from liquid.

dug /dəg/ *v. past form of* DIG.

/a/ bat, /ā/ ape, /ä/ top, /aů/ owl, /e/ elf, /ē/ eel, /i/ pin, /ī/ kite, /ō/ boat, /ȯ/ saw, /ȯi/ oil, /ů/ foot, /ü/ moon, /ch/ chair, /hw/ white, /ng/ ring, /sh/ sheep, /th/ thing, /th̲/ they, /zh/ treasure, /ə/ cup, /ər/ bird

dur•ing /dur-ing/ or /dyur-ing/ *prep.* throughout the time of: *Let's take a walk during lunchtime.*

dust /dəst/ *n.* powdery, dry earth. *v.* **dust•ed, dust•ing** 1. to remove the dust from: *Jackie dusted the table.* 2. to sprinkle with: *I dusted the cookies with sugar.*

E

ear•ly /'ər-lē/ *adv.* **ear•li•er, ear•li•est** 1. in the beginning: *We painted the house early in the spring.* 2. before the usual time: *We got to school early today.*

earth /ərth/ *n.* 1. the planet on which we live. 2. land; ground.

east /ēst/ *n.* direction of the sunrise. *adj.* area in or toward the east: *on the east side of town.*

eas•y /'ē-zē/ *adj.* **eas•i•er, eas•i•est:** not hard to do or get.

eigh•teen /ā-'tēn/ *adj.* one more than seventeen; 18.

ei•ther /'ē-t͟hər/ or /'ī-t͟hər/ *adj.* 1. one of two: *You may have either piece of fruit.* 2. each of two: *Children jumped up on either side of the cart. adv.* any more than another: *They won't work either if you won't work.*

else /els/ *adj.* other; instead: *Can someone else go, too? adv.* differently: *How else can the game be played?*

en•gine /'en-jən/ *n.* 1. machine used to power something: *The engine makes the car run.* 2. locomotive of a train.

en•joy /in-'jȯi/ *v.* **en•joyed, en•joy•ing:** to be happy with; to get pleasure from.

e•nough /i-'nəf/ *adj.* as many or as much as needed.

en•ter /'ent-ər/ *v.* **en•tered, en•ter•ing:** to go into; to come into.

es•cape /is-'kāp/ *n.* act of escaping: *His attempted escape failed. v.* **es•caped, es•cap•ing:** to get free: *The dog escaped from the yard.*

eve /ēv/ *n.* 1. the time before a special day. 2. evening.

eve•ning /'ēv-ning/ *n.* early part of the night.

ev•ery•one /'ev-rē-wən/ or /'ev-rē-ˌwən/ *pron.* each person.

ev•ery•thing /'ev-rē-ˌthing/ *pron.* all things.

ev•ery•where /'ev-rē-ˌhweər/ *adv.* in every place.

F

fair•y /'faər-ē/ *n. pl.* **fair•ies:** a tiny imaginary person with magic power.

fam•i•ly /'fam-ə-lē/ *n. pl.* **fam•i•lies** 1. people related to one another. 2. a group of people living together.

fa•mous /'fā-məs/ *adj.* well-known.

farm•er /'fär-mər/ *n.* person who owns or works on a farm.

fash•ion /'fash-ən/ *n.* style: *Fashions change quickly. v.* **fash•ioned, fash•ion•ing:** to shape or form: *He fashioned a doll out of clay.*

fas•ten /'fas-n/ *v.* **fas•tened, fas•ten•ing:** to attach or join by buckling, locking, tying, etc.: *Please fasten your seatbelt.*

feast /fēst/ *n.* 1. huge meal. 2. celebration.

feath•er /'fet͟h-ər/ *n.* one of the light, thin growths that cover a bird. *v.* **feath•ered, feath•er•ing:** to cover with feathers.

Feb•ru•ar•y /'feb-yə-ˌwer-ē/ or /'feb-rə-ˌwer-ē/ or /'feb-ə-ˌwer-ē/ *n.* second month of the year.

feel /fēl/ *v.* **felt** /felt/, **feel•ing** 1. to touch. 2. to find out through the senses: *Feel how warm the sand is.* 3. to be aware of: *I felt the cool wind on my face.*

felt /felt/ *v. past form of* FEEL.

fence /fens/ *n.* something, often of wood or wire, used to enclose an area or to prevent escape. *v.* **fenced, fenc•ing:** to put a fence around.

field /fēld/ *n.* large, open piece of land: *a wheat field; a baseball field.*

fif•teen /fif-'tēn/ *adj.* one more than fourteen; 15.

fif•ty /'fif-tē/ *adj.* five times ten; 50.

fin•ger /'fing-gər/ *n.* one of the five slim divisions that end the hand. *v.* **fin•gered, fin•ger•ing:** to touch or handle with the fingers: *Don't finger the glass.*

fin•ish /'fin-ish/ *n.* 1. end or goal: *Mandy was the first to reach the finish.* 2. treatment given a surface: *The finish of the table was scratched. v.* **fin•ished, fin•ish•ing** 1. to end; to complete. 2. to smooth, shine, or paint a surface: *Jay finished the chair with varnish.*

fire•place /'fīr-ˌplās/ *n.* place built for a fire.

fit /fit/ *v.* **fit•ted, fit•ting:** to be right or correct: *These shoes fit me. adj.* **fit•ter, fit•test** 1. healthy; in good shape. 2. right; suitable: *That dress is not fit to wear.*

fix /fiks/ *v.* **fixed, fix•ing** 1. to make firm: *Dad fixed the doghouse in place.* 2. to settle or to set: *We fixed the rules before we began playing.* 3. to mend or repair. 4. to prepare.
flew /flü/ *v. past form of* FLY.
[1]fly /flī/ *v.* **flew** /flü/, **flown** /flōn/, **fly•ing** 1. to move or pass through the air. 2. to cause to move through air: *Amy likes to fly kites.*
[2]fly /flī/ *n. pl.* **flies:** an insect with wings.
fol•low /ˈfäl-ō/ *v.* **fol•lowed, fol•low•ing:** to go or come after.
for•est /ˈfȯr-əst/ *n.* large area with trees.
for•get /fər-ˈget/ *v.* **for•got** /fər-ˈgät/, **for•got•ten** /fər-ˈgät-n/ or **for•got, for•get•ting:** to fail to remember or think of.
for•give /fər-ˈgiv/ *v.* **for•gave** /fər-ˈgāv/, **for•giv•en** /fər-ˈgiv-ən/, **for•giv•ing:** to stop feeling anger against.
for•got /fər-ˈgät/ *v. past form of* FORGET.
fort /fōrt/ *n.* strong building, usually with a high outer wall, that can be defended against an enemy.
fourth /fōrth/ *n.* one of four equal parts. *adj.* next after the third.
free /frē/ *v.* **freed, free•ing:** to set free. *adj.* **fre•er** /ˈfrē-ər/, **fre•est** /frē-əst/ 1. not under another's control. 2. having no cost or fee: *The first lesson is free.*
freeze /frēz/ *v.* **froze** /frōz/, **fro•zen** /ˈfrōz-n/, **freez•ing** 1. to turn into ice. 2. to become fixed or still: *Freeze in your tracks.*
fresh /fresh/ *adj.* new; not stale.
fry /frī/ *v.* **fried, fry•ing:** to cook in fat or oil.
fur /fər/ *n.* 1. coat of hair covering an animal. 2. clothes made of fur.

G

ghost /gōst/ *n.* spirit of a dead person.
glass /glas/ *n.* 1. breakable material that can usually be seen through. 2. anything made of glass: *Do you have juice in your glass? adj.* made of glass: *a glass dish.*
goat /gōt/ *n.* small, horned animal related to sheep but quicker and stronger.
God /gäd/ *n.* the Being who made and rules the world.
gold /gōld/ *n.* valuable yellow metal. *adj.* of the yellow color of gold.
grand /grand/ *adj.* large; great; important.
grand•fa•ther /ˈgrand-ˌfä-t̲h̲ər/ *n.* father of a person's father or mother.
grand•ma /ˈgrand-ˌmä/ or /ˈgrand-ˌmȯ/ *n.* grandmother.
grand•moth•er /ˈgrand-ˌmət̲h̲-ər/ *n.* mother of a person's father or mother.
grand•pa /ˈgrand-ˌpä/ or /ˈgrand-ˌpȯ/ *n.* grandfather.
grew /grü/ *v. past form of* GROW.
grow /grō/ *v.* **grew** /grü/, **grown** /grōn/, **grow•ing** 1. to become bigger; to increase: *Our pup has grown so fast.* 2. to live: *Cacao trees don't grow in the cold North.*
[1]gum /gəm/ *n.* flesh around the roots of teeth.
[2]gum /gəm/ *n.* 1. sticky juice from trees. 2. chewing gum.
gym /jim/ *n.* gymnasium; building or room for exercise, games, sports.

H

half /haf/ or /håf/ *n. pl.* **halves** /havz/ or /håvz/: one of two equal parts of a whole.
Hal•low•een /ˌhal-ə-ˈwēn/ or /ˌhäl-ə-ˈwēn/ *n.* the evening of October 31.
hang /hang/ *v.* **hung** /həng/ also **hanged, hang•ing:** to fasten or be fastened to something above: *Hang the picture. The light is hanging from the ceiling.*
hap•pen /ˈhap-ən/ *v.* **hap•pened, hap•pen•ing:** to take place; to occur.
has•n't /ˈhaz-nt/ has not.
have•n't /ˈhav-ənt/ have not.
health /helth/ *n.* being well; not sick: *The doctor said Stacy is in good health.*
heart /härt/ *n.* body organ that pumps the blood.
heat /hēt/ *n.* warmth; high temperature. *v.* **heat•ed, heat•ing:** to make warm or hot.
heav•y /ˈhev-ē/ *adj.* **heav•i•er, heav•i•est** 1. hard to lift or carry. 2. of more than usual weight: *I used a heavy paper to wrap the package.*
held /held/ *v. past form of* HOLD.
her•self /hər-ˈself/ or /ər-ˈself/ *pron. pl.* **them•selves** /t̲h̲əm-ˈselvz/ 1. form of the word *she* used for special emphasis: *Tammy herself repaired the chair.* 2. her own person: *She helped herself to a snack.*

/a/ bat, /ā/ ape, /ä/ top, /au̇/ owl, /e/ elf, /ē/ eel, /i/ pin, /ī/ kite, /ō/ boat, /ȯ/ saw, /ȯi/ oil, /u̇/ foot, /ü/ moon, /ch/ chair, /hw/ white, /ng/ ring, /sh/ sheep, /th/ thing, /t̲h̲/ they, /zh/ treasure, /ə/ cup, /ər/ bird

he's /hēz/ or /ēz/ 1. he is. 2. he has.
high·way /ˈhī-ˌwā/ *n.* main road.
him·self /him-ˈself/ or /im-ˈself/ *pron. pl.* **them·selves** /t͟həm-ˈselvz/ 1. form of the word *he* used for special emphasis: *David made his bed himself.* 2. his own person: *He got himself a piece of pie.*
his·to·ry /ˈhis-tə-rē/ *n. pl.* **his·to·ries:** past events.
hold /hōld/ *v.* **held** /held/, **hold·ing** 1. to keep a grasp of: *Please hold the dog.* 2. to contain: *How much milk does this glass hold?* 3. to stay fastened: *Will the glue hold?*
hole /hōl/ *n.* open or hollow place.
hol·i·day /ˈhäl-ə-ˌdā/ *n.* day of enjoyment or freedom from work or school.
hon·ey /ˈhən-ē/ *n.* sticky, sweet liquid, good to eat, that bees make from flowers.
hook /hu̇k/ *n.* curved object used for hanging things on or for catching things. *v.* **hooked, hook·ing:** to catch with a hook: *Martha hooked a big fish.*
horn /hȯrn/ *n.* 1. hard, curved growth on the heads of cattle, sheep, goats and some other animals. 2. anything shaped like a horn. 3. musical instrument.
ho·tel /hō-ˈtel/ *n.* building that has rooms and food for travelers.
hour /au̇r/ *n.* 1. sixty minutes of time. 2. time of day.
huge /hyüj/ *adj.* very large.
hun·dred /ˈhən-drəd/ *n.* ten times ten; 100.
hung /həng/ *v. past form of* HANG.
hun·gry /ˈhəng-grē/ *adj.* **hun·gri·er, hun·gri·est:** needing or wanting food.
hur·ry /ˈhər-ē/ *n. pl.* **hur·ries:** quick movement or action; haste: *They finished dinner in a hurry. v.* **hur·ried, hur·ry·ing:** to send or move quickly.

I

inch /inch/ *n.* measure of length: *There are twelve inches in a foot. v.* **inched, inch·ing:** to move slowly: *The acrobat inched along the tightrope.*
in·stead /in-ˈsted/ *adv.* in place of: *Ginny will go instead of Nicole.*
in·ter·est·ing /ˈin-trəs-ting/ or /int-ə-rəs-ting/ *adj.* holding one's attention.
in·vite /in-ˈvīt/ *v.* **in·vit·ed, in·vit·ing:** to ask someone to join in or with: *The teacher invited me to take a turn.*
is·n't /ˈiz-nt/ is not.
I've /īv/ I have.

J

jail /jāl/ *n.* prison. *v.* **jailed, jail·ing:** to put in jail: *The robber was jailed for breaking the law.*
Jan·u·ar·y /ˈjan-yə-ˌwer-ē/ *n.* first month of the year.
jet /jet/ *n.* 1. stream of liquid forced from an opening: *Jets of water shot from the fountain.* 2. jet airplane. *v.* **jet·ted, jet·ting** 1. to shoot or pour forth. 2. to travel by jet airplane.
job /jäb/ *n.* 1. particular piece of work: *Kris gave me a job to do in the garden.* 2. regular work or duty: *Ms. Wolfe has a teaching job.*
join /jȯin/ *v.* 1. to come, bring, or put together. 2. to come into the company of: *He joined us for dinner.* 3. to become a member of.
Ju·ly /ju̇-ˈlī/ *n.* seventh month of the year.
June /jün/ *n.* sixth month of the year.
[1]**junk** /jəngk/ *n.* waste; trash.
[2]**junk** /jəngk/ *n.* Chinese sailing ship.

K

[1]**kid** /kid/ *n.* 1. baby goat. 2. young child.
[2]**kid** /kid/ *v.* **kid·ded, kid·ding:** to tease or trick.
kitch·en /ˈkich-ən/ *n.* separate room in which food is cooked.
knee /nē/ *n.* joint in the middle of the leg.
knife /nīf/ *n. pl.* **knives** /nīvz/: sharp cutting blade fastened to a handle. *v.* **knifed, knif·ing:** to stab or cut with a knife.

L

la·dy /ˈlād-ē/ *n. pl.* **la·dies** 1. woman. 2. woman of high rank.
lamb /lam/ *n.* young sheep.
laugh /laf/ or /läf/ *n.* act or noise of laughing. *v.* **laughed, laugh·ing:** to smile and make sounds from the throat showing amusement or joy.

lawn /lȯn/ *n.* area of land with closely cut grass.

[1]lay /lā/ *v.* **laid** /lād/, **lay·ing:** to put or set down: *He laid the coat on the couch.*

[2]lay /lā/ *v. past form of* LIE.

[1]lead /lēd/ *n.* first; at the front: *She took the lead. v.* **led** /led/, **lead·ing** 1. to show the way. 2. to go a certain way: *The northern route leads to Rockland.* 3. to be first: *Kate leads the group in math.*

[2]lead /led/ *n.* heavy gray metal.

leaf /lēf/ *n. pl.* **leaves** /lēvz/ 1. one of the green parts of a plant that grows from a stem or the roots. 2. sheet of paper. *v.* **leafed, leaf·ing:** to turn the pages of a book: *Tim is leafing through his new book.*

[1]league /lēg/ *n.* group of people or nations joined to help one another.

[2]league /lēg/ *n.* unit of measure: *The water is only two leagues deep at this point.*

leaves /lēvz/ *n. pl. of* LEAF.

led /led/ *v. past form of* LEAD.

less /les/ *n.* smaller amount. *adj.* smaller; not so much.

li·brar·y /'lī-ˌbrer-ē/ *n. pl.* **li·brar·ies:** collection of books.

[1]lie /lī/ *n.* something said that is not true. *v.* **lied, ly·ing:** to make an untrue statement knowingly.

[2]lie /lī/ *v.* **lay** /lā/, **lain** /lān/, **ly·ing** /'lī-ing/ 1. to stretch out flat: *Lie on the beach.* 2. to be or stay in a place: *Your ring is lying on the table.*

life /līf/ *n. pl.* **lives** /līvz/: time during which a person, animal, or plant is living.

list /list/ *n.* names or items arranged one after another: *I have the list of players. v.* **list·ed, list·ing:** to make a record or list: *I listed the names of all players.*

lis·ten /'lis-n/ *v.* **lis·tened, lis·ten·ing:** to hear or try to hear.

load /lōd/ *n.* something carried: *Her van has a load of firewood. v.* **load·ed, load·ing:** to put in or put on for carrying: *We loaded up the car.*

loose /lüs/ *v.* **loosed, loos·ing:** to free: *Lynn let the bird loose after its wing healed. adj.* **loos·er, loos·est:** not fastened; not tight.

luck /lək/ *n.* chance or fortune.

M

mag·ic /'maj-ik/ *n.* secret or mysterious charms and powers. *adj.* having magic: *a magic wand.*

map /map/ *n.* flat drawing or chart showing features of the earth or skies.

March /märch/ *n.* third month of the year.

mar·ry /'mar-ē/ *v.* **mar·ried, mar·ry·ing** 1. to join two people as husband and wife. 2. to become a husband or a wife.

[1]match /mach/ *n.* 1. two persons or things that are alike or equal: *My socks are a match.* 2. contest or game: *We watched the wrestling match. v.* **matched, match·ing:** to find the equal of or one exactly like: *I hope I can match the color.*

[2]match /mach/ *n.* short piece of material tipped with a mixture that lights when scratched.

math /math/ *n.* mathematics.

May /mā/ *n.* fifth month of the year.

may·be /'mā-bē/ *adv.* possibly; perhaps.

meal /mēl/ *n.* food served or eaten at one time.

mess /mes/ *n.* 1. dirty; not neat; not in order: *This place is a mess.* 2. confusion: *Our first game was such a mess. v.* **messed, mess·ing:** to make dirty or untidy: *Why did you mess up my room?*

mice /mīs/ *n. pl. of* MOUSE.

mi·cro·scope /'mī-krə-ˌskōp/ *n.* instrument with a lens used to see an extremely small object.

mid·dle /'mid-l/ *n.* center: *I want to be in the middle. adj.* in between: *Take the middle seat.*

mid·night /'mid-ˌnīt/ *n.* twelve o'clock at night.

might·y /'mīt-ē/ *adj.* **might·i·er, might·i·est:** powerful; strong; great.

mind /mīnd/ *n.* part of a person that thinks and feels. *v.* **mind·ed, mind·ing:** to pay attention to; to watch: *Mind your manners.*

[1]min·ute /'min-ət/ *n.* sixty seconds.

[2]mi·nute /mī-'nüt/ or /mə-'nüt/ or /mī-'nyüt/ *adj.* very small; tiny: *The Earth is a minute part of the universe.*

mir·ror /'mir-ər/ *n.* surface that reflects an image.

/a/ bat, /ā/ ape, /ä/ top, /au̇/ owl, /e/ elf, /ē/ eel, /i/ pin, /ī/ kite, /ō/ boat, /ȯ/ saw, /ȯi/ oil, /u̇/ foot, /ü/ moon, /ch/ chair, /hw/ white, /ng/ ring, /sh/ sheep, /th/ thing, /t͟h/ they, /zh/ treasure, /ə/ cup, /ər/ bird

Mis·ter /'mis-tər/ *n.* title used before a man's name.

mon·key /'məng-kē/ *n. pl.* **mon·keys:** furry animal, generally living in tropical lands, that can walk upright. *v.* **mon·keyed, mon·key·ing:** to fool or play with: *Don't monkey with the light switch.*

month /mənth/ *n.* one of the twelve divisions of a year.

moss /mȯs/ *n.* small, soft, flowerless plant that clings in patches to the ground, rocks, or trees.

most·ly /'mōst-lē/ *adv.* for the most part; mainly.

moth·er /'məth-ər/ *n. poss.* **moth·er's:** female parent.

moun·tain /'maůnt-n/ *n.* 1. very high hill. 2. large amount or pile of anything: *a mountain of homework.*

mouse /maůs/ *n. pl.* **mice:** furry, gray animal that looks like a rat but is smaller.

mouth /maůth/ *n. pl.* **mouths** /maůthz/ 1. opening through which a person or animal takes food and talks or makes noises. 2. opening in something: *We entered the mouth of the cave.*

mov·ie /'mü-vē/ *n.* motion picture.

my·self /mī-'self/ or /mə-'self/ *pron. pl.* **our·selves** /aůr-'selvz/ or /är-'selvz/ 1. form of the word *I* used for special emphasis: *I will do it myself.* 2. your own person: *I bought myself a candy bar.*

N

nail / nāl/ *n.* 1. thin, pointed piece of metal used to hold things together. 2. fingernail. *v.* **nailed, nail·ing:** to fasten with a nail.

nap /nap/ *n.* short sleep. *v.* **napped, nap·ping:** to take a short sleep.

near·ly /'niər-lē/ *adv.* almost: *It's nearly time for lunch.*

news·pa·per /'nüz-ˌpā-pər/ or /'nyüz-ˌpā-pər/ *n.* daily or weekly paper of current events and other information.

no·bod·y /'nō-ˌbäd-ē/ *n. pl.* **no·bod·ies:** person of no importance. *pron.* no one.

noise /nȯiz/ *n.* 1. unpleasant sound. 2. any sound: *I thought I heard a noise downstairs.*

noon /nün/ *n.* 12 o'clock in the day.

north /nȯrth/ *n.* direction left as you face a rising sun. *adj.* at or toward the north: *the north side of town.*

note /nōt/ *n.* 1. very short letter. 2. musical sound. 3. written reminder. *v.* **not·ed, not·ing:** to take notice of: *He noted the whispers at the back of the room.*

noth·ing /'nəth-ing/ *n.* zero. *pron.* not a thing.

No·vem·ber /nō-'vem-bər/ *n.* eleventh month of the year.

nurse /nərs/ *n.* person trained to take care of the sick. *v.* **nursed, nurs·ing** 1. to care for the sick. 2. to treat carefully: *Juan nursed his sore arm.*

O

oak /ōk/ *n.* hardwood tree having acorns, or the wood from that tree.

o·cean /'ō-shən/ *n.* 1. great body of salt water that covers almost three fourths of the earth. 2. one of the four main parts, the Arctic Ocean, the Pacific Ocean, the Atlantic Ocean, or the Indian Ocean.

o'·clock /ə-'kläk/ *adv.* of the clock.

Oc·to·ber /äk-'tō-bər/ *n.* tenth month of the year.

of·ten /'ȯf-ən/ or /'ȯf-tən/ *adv.* many times.

oil /ȯil/ *n.* greasy liquid used for fuel, cooking, lubricating. *v.* **oiled, oil·ing:** to put oil on or in something.

or·ange /'ȯr-inj/ *n.* 1. round, reddish-yellow, juicy fruit. 2. reddish-yellow color.

oth·er /'əth-ər/ *adj.* 1. additional, more: *Other students will be here.* 2. different: *I want to go some other day.* 3. being the one left: *Give me the other piece.* *pron.* another or a different person or thing: *Tracy helps others.*

P

pack /pak/ *n.* 1. bundle of things tied together. 2. group or number together: *Wolves run in packs.* *v.* **packed, pack·ing** 1. to put in a box, suitcase, bundle, or the like: *Please pack the glasses carefully.* 2. to crowd together: *The people were packed into the bus.*

[1]**page** /pāj/ *n.* one side of a sheet of paper.

²page /pāj/ *n.* 1. person employed to deliver messages or to run errands. 2. youth in the Middle Ages who was preparing for knighthood: *Sir Gawain arrived with his page.* *v.* **paged, pag • ing:** to try to locate a person by having the person's name called in a group or building: *Tony Miller is being paged over the loudspeaker.*

paid /pād/ *v. past form of* PAY.

pants /pants/ *n.* trousers.

pass / pas/ *n.* 1. written permit to go or come; free ticket: *I had a pass for the circus.* 2. throw of a ball: *The pass to Archie was completed.* 3. path through a mountain range. *v.* **passed, pass • ing** 1. to go through; to go by: *We passed the candy store.* 2. to hand from one to another: *Please pass the salt.*

past /past/ *n.* time that has gone by. *adj.* gone by or ended: *The past week has been busy. adv.* by: *The motorcycles zoomed past.*

patch /pach/ *n.* 1. piece of material put on something to mend or cover it. 2. small piece or area unlike its surroundings: *There was a patch of green showing through the snow. v.* **patched, patch • ing:** to mend or cover.

pay /pā/ *v.* **paid** /pād/, **pay • ing** 1. to give money for: *Pay for your ticket.* 2. to be worthwhile: *It pays to listen carefully.*

pea /pē/ *n. pl.* **peas:** small, round seed that grows in a pod.

pear /paər/ *n.* sweet, juicy fruit rounded at one end and smaller near its stem.

pen • ny /'pen-ē/ *n. pl.* **pen • nies** /'pen-ēz/: U.S. and Canadian coin worth one cent.

per • son /'pərs-n/ *n.* human being.

phone /fōn/ *n.* telephone. *v.* **phoned, phon • ing:** to call on the telephone.

pic • nic /'pik-ˌnik/ *n.* outdoor party with food.

pipe /pīp/ *n.* 1. tube through which a liquid or gas flows. 2. tube with a small bowl at one end for smoking tobacco or for blowing bubbles. *v.* **piped, pip • ing:** to carry a liquid or gas through pipes.

plain /plān/ *n.* flat stretch of land: *Cattle grazed on the plains. adj.* 1. easy to understand: *The instructions are plain enough.* 2. not fancy; simple: *plain yellow curtains.*

plan /plan/ *n.* drawing or scheme for doing something. *v.* **planned, plan • ning:** to think out a way of doing something.

¹plane /plān/ *n.* 1. level or flat surface. 2. airplane.

²plane /plān/ *n.* tool with a blade for smoothing wood. *v.* **planed, plan • ing:** to smooth with a plane.

plan • et /'plan-ət/ *n.* one of the heavenly bodies that moves around the sun: *Mars is a planet.*

play • ground /'plā-ˌgraůnd/ *n.* area where children can play.

plen • ty /'plent-ē/ *n.* full supply; enough.

pock • et /'päk-ət/ *n.* 1. small bag sewed into clothing. 2. place or thing like a pocket: *The airplane hit an air pocket.* *v.* **pock • et • ed, pock • et • ing:** to put in a pocket. *adj.* small enough to fit in a pocket: *Kathy has a pocket camera.*

po • em /'pō-əm/ *n.* piece of writing in verse.

point /pȯint/ *n.* 1. sharp end. 2. dot. 3. detail; small part: *There is another point to consider.* 4. used in scoring. *v.* **point • ed, point • ing:** to aim or indicate something.

po • lice /pə-'lēs/ *n. pl.* **police:** department of government that keeps law and order. *v.* **po • liced, po • lic • ing:** to keep in order.

po • lice • man /pə-'lēs-mən/ *n. pl.* **po • lice • men** /pə-'lēs-mən/: member of the police force.

pop /päp/ *n.* 1. short, quick, explosive sound. 2. soft drink. *v.* **popped, pop • ping** 1. to make a short, quick, explosive sound. 2. to cause something to burst: *Joey popped his balloon.*

porch /pōrch/ *n.* covered entrance to a building.

¹post /pōst/ *n.* pole; piece of timber, metal or such fixed upright. *v.* **post • ed, post • ing:** to fasten or put up a notice: *The coach posted the list of players.*

²post /pōst/ *n.* place where someone is stationed for duty. *v.* **post • ed, post • ing:** to assign someone to a position: *Guards were posted at the gate.*

³post /pōst/ *n.* mail: *I shall send the package by post. v.* **post • ed, post • ing:** to mail something: *I posted the letter.*

pot /pät/ *n.* container usually used for cooking.

/a/ bat, /ā/ ape, /ä/ top, /aů/ owl, /e/ elf, /ē/ eel, /i/ pin, /ī/ kite, /ō/ boat, /ȯ/ saw, /ȯi/ oil, /ů/ foot, /ü/ moon, /ch/ chair, /hw/ white, /ng/ ring, /sh/ sheep, /th/ thing, /t͟h/ they, /zh/ treasure, /ə/ cup, /ər/ bird

po·ta·to /pə-'tāt-ō/ *n. pl.* **po·ta·toes:** round or oval shaped vegetable that grows underground.

[1]pound /paůnd/ *n.* 1. 16 ounces. 2. unit of money in some countries.

[2]pound /paůnd/ *v.* **pound·ed, pound·ing:** to strike or beat again and again: *Jeff pounded on the door.*

[1]pres·ent /'prez-nt/ *n.* now, not past or future: *He lives only for the present. adj.* not absent: *Everyone is present today.*

[2]pre·sent /'prez-nt/ *n.* gift. /pri-'zent/ *v.* **pre·sent·ed, pre·sent·ing** 1. to introduce one person to another. 2. to bring before the public: *We'll present our play to the rest of the school.* 3. to give.

prin·cess /'prin-səs/ or /'prin-ˌses/ *n.* 1. daughter of a king or queen. 2. wife of a prince.

prob·a·bly /'präb-ə-blē/ *adv.* very likely.

prob·lem /'präb-ləm/ *n.* question or difficult matter.

pro·gram /'prō-ˌgram/ or /'prō-grəm/ *n.* 1. outline of a performance: *The actors and actresses are listed in the program.* 2. performance: *We watched a good TV program. v.* **pro·grammed** or **pro·gramed, pro·gram·ming** or **pro·gram·ing:** to put instructions into a computer: *Alison programed the computer to solve the problem.*

pur·ple /'pər-pəl/ *n.* mixture of the colors blue and red.

Q

queen /kwēn/ *n.* 1. woman ruler of a kingdom. 2. wife of a king.

quick /kwik/ *adj.* fast: *Willie made a quick trip to the store.*

qui·et /'kwī-ət/ *adj.* making very little or no noise. *v.* **qui·et·ed, qui·et·ing:** to calm or to quiet: *Can you quiet the dog?*

quit /kwit/ *v.* **quit, quit·ting:** to stop; to give up; to leave.

quite /kwīt/ *adv.* completely; entirely: *I am not quite done with my dinner.*

R

rain·y /'rā-nē/ *adj.* **rain·i·er, rain·i·est:** having much rain.

raise /rāz/ *v.* **raised, raising** 1. to lift. 2. to bring up; to help grow: *Marie raised carrots this year.* 3. to increase.

ranch /ranch/ *n.* large farm for raising animals such as cattle and horses. *v.* **ranched, ranch·ing:** to work on a ranch.

rang /rang/ *v. past form of* RING.

rath·er /'rath-ər/ *adv.* 1. more willingly: *I would rather have milk than juice.* 2. instead: *Don't buy the brown one but rather the orange.*

reach /rēch/ *v.* **reached, reach·ing** 1. to arrive at: *We will reach Chicago soon.* 2. to touch or get hold of: *I cannot reach the boxes on that shelf.*

read·y /'red-ē/ *adj.* **read·i·er, read·i·est:** prepared for something: *Are you ready to talk with me?*

re·al /'rē-əl/ *adj.* 1. actual; true. 2. what it seems to be: *a real diamond.*

re·al·ly /'rē-ə-lē/ *adv.* actually; truly.

rea·son /'rēz-n/ *n.* 1. cause. 2. ability to think: *Man uses reason. v.* **rea·soned, rea·son·ing:** to use the mind or to persuade: *Try to reason with him to get him to come.*

re·cess /'rē-ˌses/ or /ri-'ses/ *n.* 1. short break from work. 2. small hollow or indented place: *A table might fit nicely in that recess. v.* **re·cessed, re·cess·ing:** to take a short break.

rein·deer /'rān-ˌdiər/ *n. pl.* **rein·deer:** large antlered deer that lives in the cold north.

re·mem·ber /ri-'mem-bər/ *v.* **re·mem·bered, re·mem·ber·ing:** to think of again; to keep in mind.

re·port /ri-'pōrt/ *n.* statement, written or spoken, about something: *Lennie gave a report on baseball. v.* **re·port·ed, re·port·ing** 1. to give an account of. 2. to make a charge against: *He was reported for fighting.* 3. to appear for duty: *The sailor reported to the captain.*

rice /rīs/ *n.* grain of a cereal plant grown in warm climates for food.

rich /rich/ *adj.* 1. having much money, land, property, etc. 2. expensive: *rich jewels and clothing.* 3. containing much sugar, fat, flavoring: *a rich dessert.*

ride /rīd/ *n.* trip on something. *v.* **rode** /rōd/, **rid·den** /'rid-n/, **rid·ing** /'rīd-ing/: to sit on or in something that moves.

right /rīt/ *n.* just or moral claim: *I have a right to my opinion. adj.* 1. just; lawful. 2. correct; true.

[1]ring /ring/ *n.* 1. band, usually of metal, worn as an ornament. 2. something having the shape of a circle: *a smoke ring.* 3. place for public showings or contests: *a circus ring.* 4. sound made as by a bell: *The ring of the phone startled me. v.* **ringed, ring • ing** 1. to make or put a circle around. 2. to toss a ring, horseshoe, etc. over a post: *My cousin ringed the post on the first try.*

[2]ring /ring/ *v.* **rang** /rang/, **rung** /rəng/, **ring • ing** 1. to sound a bell. 2. to sound loudly. 3. to call on the telephone.

rock • et /räk-ət/ *n.* device or vehicle that uses gases forced from its rear end as fuel.

rode /rōd/ *v. past form of* RIDE.

roll /rōl/ *n.* 1. list of names: *The teacher called the roll.* 2. small, round bread or cake. 3. anything rolled up: *Open a roll of paper towels. v.* **rolled, roll • ing:** to move by turning over and over.

[1]row /rō/ *n.* things or people in a line.

[2]row /rō/ *v.* **rowed, row • ing:** to move with oars: *At camp we learned to row a boat.*

rub • ber /'rəb-ər/ *n.* 1. stretchy material made from the juice of certain tropical plants. 2. anything made from rubber.

rule /rül/ *n.* 1. statement of how to behave. 2. reign or time of a ruler. 3. ruler for measuring or drawing lines. *v.* **ruled, rul • ing** 1. to control. 2. to give a verdict: *The court ruled on the new law.*

rul • er /'rül-ər/ *n.* 1. person who rules or governs. 2. straight strip for measuring or drawing lines.

S

sack /sak/ *n.* bag.

sad /sad/ *adj.* **sad • der, sad • dest:** unhappy.

sad • dle /'sad-l/ *n.* seat for a rider on a horse or on a bicycle. *v.* **sad • dled, sad • dling:** to put a saddle on something.

sail /sāl/ *n.* cloth that catches the wind to make a boat move. *v.* **sailed, sail • ing:** 1. to travel on water 2. to travel through the air: *The glider sailed through the air for forty minutes.*

sale /sāl/ *n.* 1. to give someone goods for money: *I made my first sale of the day.* 2. selling at lower prices than usual: *Many stores have sales on summer items at the end of summer.*

save /sāv/ *v.* **saved, sav • ing** 1. to rescue from harm. 2. to store up; to set aside: *I am saving my money to buy a hamster.*

scare /skeər/ *n.* fright: *That loud crash gave Bill a scare. v.* **scared, scar • ing:** to frighten or make afraid.

[1]seal /sēl/ *n.* sea animal that has flippers for swimming and is sometimes hunted for its fur.

[2]seal /sēl/ *n.* 1. design stamped on something to show ownership or authority: *The President put his seal on the treaty.* 2. anything used to firmly fasten or close something. *v.* **sealed, seal • ing** 1. to stamp with an official seal. 2. to close something tightly.

seat /sēt/ *n.* place to sit. *v.* **seat • ed, seat • ing** 1. to sit down: *Please be seated.* 2. to have seats for: *The lunchroom seats 100 people.*

se • cret /'sē-krət/ *n.* something hidden or not known to others: *Can you keep a secret? adj.* hidden: *The cave has a secret entrance.*

seem /sēm/ *v.* **seemed, seem • ing:** to appear to be: *You seem happy today.*

self /self/ *n. pl.* **selves** /selvz/: one's own person: *Andy seems to be his old fun-loving self today.*

sell /sel/ *v.* **sold** /sōld/, **sell • ing:** to give in return for money.

Sep • tem • ber /sep-'tem-bər/ *n.* ninth month of the year.

sev • en /'sev-ən/ *n. adj.* one more than six; 7.

sev • enth /'sev-ənth/ *adj.* next after the sixth.

sew /sō/ *v.* **sewed, sewed** or **sewn** /sōn/, **sew • ing:** to work with a needle and thread.

shape /shāp/ *n.* form; figure; outline: *We could barely see the shape of the lighthouse through the fog. v.* **shaped, shap • ing:** to form or develop something: *Bart shaped the clay into a pot.*

share /sheər/ *n.* part: *Everyone had a share of the ice cream. v.* **shared, shar • ing:** to divide up or to have a part: *We'll share the cookies.*

/a/ bat, /ā/ ape, /ä/ top, /au̇/ owl, /e/ elf, /ē/ eel, /i/ pin, /ī/ kite, /ō/ boat, /ȯ/ saw, /ȯi/ oil, /u̇/ foot, /ü/ moon, /ch/ chair, /hw/ white, /ng/ ring, /sh/ sheep, /th/ thing, /t͟h/ they, /zh/ treasure, /ə/ cup, /ər/ bird

sharp /shärp/ *adj.* 1. having a thin cutting edge or a fine point. 2. very cold: *A sharp wind blew in from the lake.* 3. quick or sudden change of direction: *Make a sharp turn to the left at the top of the hill.*

shell /shel/ *n.* 1. hard outside covering on eggs, seeds, and some kinds of animals. 2. anything that looks like or serves as a shell: *The hull of a boat is called a shell.* 3. small case filled with gunpowder to be shot from a rifle. *v.* **shelled, shell · ing:** to remove from the shell.

shirt /shərt/ *n.* piece of clothing for the upper part of the body.

shoe /shü/ *n.* outer covering for the foot, usually having a hard or stiff sole.

shoot /shüt/ *n.* new plant or part of a plant growing out: *You can see shoots coming up in our garden now. v.* **shot** /shät/, **shoot · ing** 1. to hit with a bullet, arrow, or the like. 2. to fire a gun or bow. 2. to send something quickly: *Wendy is good at shooting marbles.*

shore /shōr/ *n.* land at the edge of a body of water.

short /shȯrt/ *adj.* 1. not long: *We took a short walk.* 2. not tall: *He is short for his age.* 3. brief: *a short visit.*

should · n't /'shüd-nt/ should not.

shout /shaüt/ *n.* loud cry: *Jeremy heard a shout for help. v.* **shout · ed, shout · ing:** to call or cry loudly.

sight /sīt/ *n.* 1. ability to see: *Grandpa's sight failed as he grew older.* 2. something worth seeing: *You are a sight in that costume.* *v.* **sight · ed, sight · ing:** to see: *We sighted a deer on the hill.*

sign /sīn/ *n.* 1. any mark or movement used to stand for or point out something. 2. printed notice that has been posted: *Did you read the sign in the window?* *v.* **signed, sign · ing:** to put one's name on: *Please sign your paper.*

silk /silk/ *n.* 1. fine thread spun by silkworms. 2. thread, clothing, or anything made of this fiber.

sil · ly /'sil-ē/ *adj.* **sil · li · er, sil · li · est:** foolish; stupid.

sil · ver /'sil-vər/ *n.* 1. shiny, gray-white, precious metal. 2. anything made of this metal. 3. color of silver; gray.

sin · gle /'sing-gəl/ *adj.* only one; alone: *He didn't have a single penny left.*

sir /sər/ *n.* title of respect used in talking to a man.

size /sīz/ *n.* 1. amount of space a thing takes up: *Look at the size of this fish!* 2. one in a number of measurements: *What size is this coat?*

skate /skāt/ *n.* shoelike frame with blades or wheels used for gliding or moving. *v.* **skat · ed, skat · ing:** to move on skates or slide as if on skates.

sleep /slēp/ *n.* rest of body and mind. *v.* **slept** /slept/, **sleep · ing:** to rest one's body and mind: *Go to sleep early tonight.*

sleep · y /'slē-pē/ *adj.* **sleep · i · er, sleep · i · est** 1. ready to fall asleep. 2. quiet; not active: *This is a sleepy neighborhood on Sunday afternoons.*

sleigh /slā/ *n.* carriage on runners for use on ice or snow.

slept /slept/ *v. past form of* SLEEP.

slid /slid/ *v. past form of* SLIDE.

slide /slīd/ *n.* smooth, usually slanted surface for sliding on. *v.* **slid** /slid/, **slid · ing** /slīd-ing/ 1. to move smoothly and quietly over a surface. 2. to slip: *Someone slid a note under our door.*

slip /slip/ *v.* **slipped, slip · ping** 1. to slide or move easily: *This piece should slip into place easily.* 2. to move out of place: *The glass slipped from her hand.*

slow /slō/ *v.* **slowed, slow · ing:** to make slow: *I slowed down the car. adj.* taking a long time: *Willy is the slowest horse we have.*

smart /smärt/ *adj.* clever; bright.

smell /smel/ *n.* scent or odor: *I like the smell of pine trees. v.* **smelled** /smeld/ or **smelt** /smelt/, **smell · ing** 1. to become aware of through the use of the nose. 2. to give out a smell: *Dinner certainly smells good.*

smile /smīl/ *n.* expression showing pleasure or amusement: *Her smile made everyone happy. v.* **smiled, smil · ing:** to curve the mouth upward because of pleasure or amusement: *Mother smiled when we gave her some flowers.*

smoke /smōk/ *n.* cloud formed from anything burning. *v.* **smoked, smok · ing:** to send out smoke: *The damp wood made our fire smoke too much.*

snake /snāk/ *n.* long, thin, legless reptile.

[1]**sock** /säk/ *n. pl.* **socks** or **sox** /säks/: cloth covering for the foot, sometimes extending up to the knee.

²sock /säk/ *n.* hard blow. *v.* **socked, sock • ing:** to strike or hit hard: *Billy really socked that ball.*

soft /sȯft/ *adj.* 1. not hard or stiff: *Puppy fur is very soft.* 2. quiet; gentle: *The radio played soft music.*

soft • en /ˈsȯf-ən/ *v.* **soft • ened, soft • en • ing:** to make or become soft.

sold /sōld/ *v. past form of* SELL.

some • bod • y /ˈsəm-ˌbäd-ē/ *pron.* person not known or named.

some • where /ˈsəm-ˌhweər/ *adv.* place not known or named.

son /sən/ *n.* male child of a parent or parents.

sore /sōr/ *n.* injury or painful place on the body: *Sara has a sore where she fell on her knee. adj.* painful: *Our dog limps on his sore leg.*

space /spās/ *n.* 1. limitless area extending in all directions: *Men explore space in rocket ships.* 2. limited, measurable area: *There's space for three books on this shelf.* *v.* **spaced, spac • ing:** to fix the space of: *Please space these chairs across the front of the room.*

speak /spēk/ *v.* **spoke** /spōk/, **spo • ken** /ˈspō-kən/, **speak • ing:** to talk.

spe • cial /ˈspesh-əl/ *adj.* different from others; of a particular kind: *Manuel is my special friend.*

spell • ing /ˈspel-ing/ *n.* writing or saying of the letters of a word in order.

spend /spend/ *v.* **spent** /spent/, **spend • ing:** to use up in any manner: *Let's spend the evening at the movies.*

spent /spent/ *v. past form of* SPEND.

spi • der /ˈspīd-ər/ *n.* small wingless animal with eight legs.

¹spoke /spōk/ *n.* bar going from the center of a wheel to its rim.

²spoke /spōk/ *v. past form of* SPEAK.

spoon /spün/ *n.* kitchen instrument with small, shallow bowl at the end of a handle. *v.* **spooned, spoon • ing:** to take up in a spoon: *Mom spooned out the peas.*

sport /spōrt/ *n.* game; outdoor play: *Tennis and handball are active sports.*

spot /spät/ *n.* mark; stain; small part different from the rest: *The rain left spots on my new coat. v.* **spot • ted, spot • ting:** to mark with spots: *The rain spotted my new coat.*

spread /spred/ *n.* 1. width; extent of spreading: *The airplane's wing spread was sixty feet.* 2. covering for a bed or table: *Mom bought a new spread for the bed.* *v.* **spread, spread • ing:** to stretch out; to open out; to cover: *Please spread the cloth over the table.*

spy /spī/ *n. pl.* **spies:** person who secretly watches others. *v.* **spied, spy • ing** 1. to watch or observe secretly. 2. to perform or work as a spy. 3. to catch sight of.

squir • rel /ˈskwər-əl/ *n.* small bushy-tailed animal that usually lives in trees.

stage /stāj/ *n.* 1. raised platform. 2. one step in a process: *The first stage of our trip ended in Paris.* 3. each part of a rocket that has its own engine and fuel: *The rocket's first stage separated soon after the blast-off.* *v.* **staged, stag • ing:** to present a play or program of some kind: *Our class staged a play for the school.*

stair /staər/ *n. pl.* **stairs:** series of steps.

stand /stand/ *n.* 1. something to place things on or to put things in. 2. place or position: *The policeman took his stand at the corner to direct traffic.* 3. a stop or a halt to make a defense: *The soldiers took a stand at the edge of the forest. v.* **stood** /stu̇d/, **stand • ing** 1. to be on or to rise to one's feet. 2. to set upright or to be set upright: *Stand the crates in the corner.* 3. to be in a certain place: *The tree stands at the top of the hill.* 4. to undergo or to be subjected to: *to stand trial.*

star /stär/ *n.* 1. any of the bright bodies, except the planets, seen in the sky at night. 2. figure usually having five or six points. 3. actor, actress, singer, comedian, etc. *v.* **starred, star • ring:** to be a leading performer: *My favorite singer starred in that movie.*

state /stāt/ *n.* 1. condition of a person or thing: *He is in a calm state now.* 2. group of people in one area under one government: *Alaska is our largest state. v.* **stat • ed, stat • ing:** to say or tell: *Everyone had to state his or her name.*

sta • tion /ˈstā-shən/ *n.* 1. place to stand: *Please take up a station by the door.* 2. building or place used for a special purpose: *We live near a fire station.*

/a/ bat, /ā/ ape, /ä/ top, /au̇/ owl, /e/ elf, /ē/ eel, /i/ pin, /ī/ kite, /ō/ boat, /ȯ/ saw, /ȯi/ oil, /u̇/ foot, /ü/ moon, /ch/ chair, /hw/ white, /ng/ ring, /sh/ sheep, /th/ thing, /th/ they, /zh/ treasure, /ə/ cup, /ər/ bird

v. **sta·tioned, sta·tion·ing:** to assign to a place: *The Navy stationed my brother in Florida.*

step /step/ *n.* 1. movement of a foot in walking, running, dancing. 2. each stair in a stairway. 3. stage in a process: *Follow the directions step by step. v.* **stepped, step·ping** 1. to move by walking, running, dancing. 2. to push down with the foot: *Bobby stepped on the burning match.*

stick /stik/ *n.* 1. small branch or twig. 2. something in the shape of a stick: *a stick of candy. v.* **stuck** /stək/, **stick·ing** 1. to make a hole with a pointed object; to stab. 2. to attach; to be fastened. 3. to become fixed or blocked: *The wheels became stuck in the deep sand.* 4. to put into a particular place or position: *Stick the papers in this drawer.* 5. to puzzle; to confuse: *I'm stuck on this problem.*

stock /stäk/ *n.* 1. supply: *This store has a large stock of candy.* 2. shares in a company: *We own some oil stock. v.* **stocked, stock·ing:** to put in a supply of: *The farmer stocked the pond with fish.*

stood /stu̇d/ *v. past form of* STAND.

strange /strānj/ *adj.* **strang·er, strang·est:** not familiar; unusual.

stuck /stək/ *v. past form of* STICK.

stud·y /'stəd-ē/ *n. pl.* **stud·ies:** attempt to learn by reading or thinking: *Mel made a study of the Civil War. v.* **stud·ied, stud·y·ing:** to examine or think about in an effort to learn: *Nita studied history.*

such /səch/ *adj.* of a certain kind: *Let's get some fruit such as apples. pron.* that sort of thing, person, or group: *We can swim, play softball, ride horses, and such.*

sud·den /'səd-n/ *adj.* not expected; hurried; quick.

sug·ar /'shu̇g-ər/ *n.* sweet substance made from sugar cane or sugar beets. *v.* **sug·ared, sug·ar·ing:** to add sugar to something: *Mom already sugared her tea.*

suit /süt/ *n.* 1. set of clothes: *a new plaid suit.* 2. case in a law court: *a suit for damages. v.* **suit·ed, suit·ing:** to please; to satisfy: *Do the new rules suit you?*

sun·ny /'sən-ē/ *adj.* **sun·ni·er, sun·ni·est** 1. having a lot of sunshine. 2. bright; pleasant; cheerful: *Gloria has a sunny smile.*

sure /shu̇r/ *adj.* **sur·er, sur·est:** certain: *Are you sure of your answer?*

sur·prise /sər-'prīz/ *n.* something unexpected: *The surprise was a new bike. v.* **sur·prised, sur·pris·ing:** to do something unexpected: *We surprised Mom with a party.*

sweet /swēt/ *adj.* 1. having a taste like sugar or honey. 2. fresh; not sour: *Perfume has a sweet smell.* 3. pleasant; dear: *a sweet baby.*

T

tail /tāl/ *n.* 1. back part of an animal that extends beyond the main part. 2. rear part of something: *My kite lost its tail in the high wind.*

take /tāk/ *v.* **took** /tu̇k/, **tak·en** /'tā-kən/, **tak·ing:** to get hold of: *Did you take a cookie?*

tea /tē/ *n.* drink made from the dried leaves of a shrub.

[1]**tear** /tiər/ *n.* drop of liquid that comes from the eye.

[2]**tear** /taər/ *n.* ripped or torn place: *You have a tear in your jacket. v.* **tore** /tōr/, **torn** /tōrn/, **tear·ing:** to pull apart by force, to rip: *Lisa tore the paper.*

teeth /tēth/ *n. pl. of* TOOTH.

tel·e·phone /'tel-ə-ˌfōn/ *n.* instrument for sending sounds from a distance. *v.* **tel·e·phoned, tel·e·phon·ing:** to use the telephone.

thank·ful /thangk-fəl/ *adj.* feeling thanks; grateful: *The farmers were thankful for the rain.*

Thanks·giv·ing /thangks-'giv-ing/ *n.* fourth Thursday in November set aside to give thanks to God for all we have.

there's /t͟haərz/ there is.

thin /thin/ *adj.* **thin·ner, thin·nest:** not thick: *The ice is thin in this spot.*

thir·ty /'thərt-ē/ *adj.* three times ten; 30.

though /t͟hō/ *adv.* however: *He will not be here for long though. conj.* in spite of the fact that: *Jody takes her medicine though she does not like it.*

thou·sand /'thau̇z-nd/ *n.* ten hundreds; 1,000. *adj.* being 1,000.

threw /thrü/ *v. past form of* THROW.

through /thrü/ *adj.* 1. going from one point to another without change: *through traffic.* 2. finished: *Are you through with dinner yet? adv.* from the beginning to the end: *Kris got through the report by 3:00. prep.* 1. from one side to the other: *through the mountain pass.* 2. among: *We walked through the flowers.* 3. during a whole period of time: *through the morning.*

throw /thrō/ *n.* act of throwing: *The pitcher's throw was wild. v.* **threw** /thrü/, **thrown** /thrōn/, **throw·ing:** to fling; to toss; to hurl: *Throw the ball to Jan.*

tick·et /'tik-ət/ *n.* 1. card serving as a pass for admission: *tickets for the game.* 2. court summons given to a person who breaks a traffic law: *The policeman gave him a speeding ticket. v.* **tick·et·ed, tick·et·ing:** to put a ticket on: *The clerks ticketed all the new stock.*

tie /tī/ *n.* 1. anything used for fastening or binding. 2. necktie. 3. one of the supports to which railroad rails are fastened. *v.* **tied, ty·ing** /'tī-ing/ or **tie·ing:** to fasten or bind: *Tie your shoestrings.*

tight /tīt/ *adj.* 1. firmly held: *Amy could not unscrew the tight lid.* 2. fitting closely: *My shoes are too tight.*

[1]till /til/ *prep.* or *conj.* until: *I will be here till noon.*

[2]till /til/ *v.* **tilled, till·ing:** to prepare land for crops; to plow: *The farmer tilled the fields.*

ti·ny /'tī-nē/ *adj.* **ti·ni·er, ti·ni·est:** very small.

[1]tip /tip/ *n.* end; point: *the tip of a pencil. v.* **tipped, tip·ping:** to put a tip on.

[2]tip /tip/ *v.* **tipped, tip·ping** 1. to slope; to slant: *The table tipped toward Randy.* 2. to overturn: *The dog tipped over his dish.*

[3]tip /tip/ *n.* 1. small gift of money: *He gave the waiter a tip.* 2. piece of information: *He gave us a tip on the best way to cook lamb chops. v.* **tipped, tip·ping** 1. to give money as a present: *We tipped the taxi driver.* 2. to give information: *My friend tipped me off about the meeting.*

to·geth·er /tə-'ge<u>th</u>-ər/ *adv.* with each other.

to·mor·row /tə-'mär-ō/ *n.* day after today. *adv.* on or for the day after today.

took /tük/ *v. past form of* TAKE.

tooth /tüth/ *n. pl.* **teeth** /tēth/ 1. one of the bonelike parts in the mouth used for biting and chewing: *The dentist cleaned my teeth today.* 2. something like a tooth: *I broke a tooth in my comb.*

to·ward /'tō-ərd/ or /tə-'wȯrd/ *prep.* in the direction of: *I walked toward the park to find Jimmy.*

track /trak/ *n.* 1. path or course for running or moving on such as a railroad track or race track. 2. mark; footprint: *The bear left tracks around the camp. v.* **tracked, track·ing** 1. to follow the tracks of: *The hunter tracked the deer.* 2. to dirty with the feet: *Don't track up the newly washed floor.*

trade /trād/ *n.* 1. business of buying and selling goods: *The United States has a large foreign trade.* 2. exchange: *We traded addresses.* 3. kind of work: *He learned the plumber's trade. v.* **trad·ed, trad·ing:** to buy and sell or to exchange.

trap /trap/ *n.* anything used to capture by surprise: *We set traps for the mice. v.* **trapped, trap·ping:** to catch by surprise: *The police trapped the robber before he could escape.*

treat /trēt/ *n.* 1. something given free by another. 2. anything that is fun or pleasant: *It is always a treat to visit the zoo. v.* **treat·ed, treat·ing** 1. act toward: *My aunt always treats me well.* 2. to supply something free for someone: *Dad treated the whole team to ice cream.*

trick /trik/ *n.* 1. something done to cheat. 2. clever act: *My dog knows many tricks. v.* **tricked, trick·ing:** to cheat or fool someone.

trou·ble /'trəb-əl/ *n.* worry: *Her troubles are many. v.* **trou·bled, trou·bling:** to disturb; to cause worry to: *I was troubled when you didn't arrive on time.*

true /trü/ *adj.* **tru·er, tru·est:** faithful; not false; honest; real.

tur·key /'tər-kē/ *n. pl.* **tur·keys:** large American bird raised for food.

twelve /twelv/ *adj.* one more than eleven; 12.

twen·ty /'twent-ē/ *n., adj.* two times ten; 20.

/a/ bat, /ā/ ape, /ä/ top, /au̇/ owl, /e/ elf, /ē/ eel, /i/ pin, /ī/ kite, /ō/ boat, /ȯ/ saw, /ȯi/ oil, /u̇/ foot, /ü/ moon, /ch/ chair, /hw/ white, /ng/ ring, /sh/ sheep, /th/ thing, /<u>th</u>/ they, /zh/ treasure, /ə/ cup, /ər/ bird

U

un • less /ən-'les/ *conj.* if not: *She'll come soon unless she missed the bus.*

up • stairs /'əp-'staərz/ *n.* upper floor of a building. *adj.* /'əp-ˌstaərz/: on an upper floor: *Hers is an upstairs room. adv.* /'əp-'staərz/: on or to a higher floor: *Please go upstairs.*

V

va • ca • tion /vā-'kā-shən/ *n.* time away from work or school. *v.* **va • ca • tioned, va • ca • tion • ing:** to take or spend time off: *We vacationed at the seashore.*

val • ley /'val-ē/ *n. pl.* **val • leys:** section of low land between hills or mountains.

voice /vȯis/ *n.* sound made through the mouth. *v.* **voiced, voic • ing:** to state or express: *Our teacher voiced her dislike for the noise.*

W

wag • on /'wag-ən/ *n.* four-wheeled vehicle used for carrying things.

wak /wāk/ *v.* **waked** or **woke** /wōk/, **waked** or **wo • ken** /'wō-kən/, **wak • ing:** to stop or cause to stop sleeping; to awaken.

wall /wȯl/ *n.* 1. side of a room. 2. solid material used to enclose an area.

war /wȯr/ *n.* 1. fight between states or nations. 2. struggle. *v.* **warred, war • ring:** to take part in a war or struggle.

wear /waər/ *n.* act of wearing. *v.* **wore** /wōr/, **worn** /wōrn/, **wear • ing** 1. to use as clothing. 2. to use up or to damage through use: *These steps are so worn that they sag.*

weath • er /'weth-ər/ *n.* condition of the air. *v.* **weath • ered, weath • er • ing:** to survive against bad conditions: *The ship weathered the storm.*

west /west/ *n.* direction of the sunset. *adj.* in or toward that direction: *She lives on the west side of town. adv.* to the west: *Walk west one mile.*

wheat /hwēt/ *n.* cereal grain from which flour is made.

wheel /hwēl/ *n.* 1. round or circular object that turns or rolls. 2. anything like a wheel: *The store had a big wheel of cheese.* *v.* **wheel • ed, wheel • ing** 1. to move something on wheels: *Mom wheeled the cart through the store.* 2. to turn quickly: *Carmen wheeled around at the noise.*

whis • tle /'hwis-əl/ *n.* instrument used for making a shrill sound. *v.* **whis • tled, whis • tling:** to make a clear, shrill noise: *The tea kettle whistled when the water boiled.*

whole /hōl/ *adj.* entire or complete.

whose /hüz/ *pron.* of whom, of which: *Whose coat is this?*

wide /wīd/*adj.* **wid • er, wid • est** 1. filling much space from side to side: *a wide river.* 2. spreading a particular distance across: *That door is thirty-six inches wide.*

wife /wīf/ *n. pl.* **wives** /wīvz/: woman who is married.

wire /wīr/*n.* threadlike metal: *There are telephone wires in our backyard. v.***wired, wir • ing** 1. to furnish with wire: *The men wired the house for electricity.* 2. to fasten together: *We wired the bundles together.* 3. to send a telegram: *We wired the news to Grandmother.*

witch /wich/ *n.* 1. woman thought to have magic powers. 2. ugly woman.

with • out /with-'au̇t/ or /with-'au̇t/ *prep.* not having; lacking: *Jon is without money.*

woke /wōk/ *v. past form of* WAKE.

wolf /wu̇lf/ *n. pl.* **wolves** /wu̇lvz/: wild animal that looks like a dog.

wom • an /'wu̇m-ən/ *n. pl.* **wom • en** /'wim-ən/: adult female.

wom • en /'wim-ən/ *n. pl. of* WOMAN.

won • der /'wən-dər/ *n.* surprising thing: *Nature has many wonders. v.* **won • dered, won • der • ing:** to be surprised or curious: *I wonder where Brad has gone.*

won't /wōnt/ will not.

wood • en /'wu̇d-n/ *adj.* made out of wood.

wore /wōr/ *v. past form of* WEAR.

worm /wərm/ *n.* small, crawling animal, usually with no legs.

worn /wōrn/ *v. past form of* WEAR.
wor • ry /'wər-ē/*n. pl.* **wor • ries:** care; uneasiness. *v.* **wor • ried, wor • ry • ing:** to feel anxious; to be uneasy: *I worried that the storm would make driving dangerous.*
would • n't /'wu̇d-nt/ would not.
wreck /rek/ *n.* destruction or ruin; accident: *The heavy snowfall caused many wrecks.* *v.* **wrecked, wreck • ing:** to ruin or destroy: *The tornado wrecked the whole town.*
wrong /rȯng/*n.* unfair or unjust act. *v.* **wronged, wrong • ing:** to harm or injure: *Since he wasn't guilty, Scott felt wronged in being accused. adj.* not right; not correct.

Y

¹yard /yärd/ *n.* 1. ground around a house or building. 2. enclosed area for business: *a navy yard.*
²yard /yärd/ *n.* three feet or thirty-six inches.
you'll /yül/ you shall; you will.
young /yəng/ adj. new in life; not old.
you're /yər/ or /yu̇r/ you are.

Z

zoo /zü/ *n. pl.* **zoos:** place where animals are cared for and displayed.

/a/ bat, /ā/ ape, /ä/ top, /au̇/ owl, /e/ elf, /ē/ eel, /i/ pin, /ī/ kite, /ō/ boat, /ȯ/ saw, /ȯi/ oil, /u̇/ foot, /ü/ moon, /ch/ chair, /hw/ white, /ng/ ring, /sh/ sheep, /th/ thing, /t̲h̲/ they, /zh/ treasure, /ə/ cup, /ər/ bird

Word Lists

Unit 1 Words

grand, son, thin, life, smart, bean, seat, rather, rubber, fry, September, bottle, aren't, whole, bought, wrote, hasn't, shouldn't, mountain, certain

Unit 2 Words

less, alike, wide, alive, pay, block, dry, baseball, spider, cabin, bike, brighter, skate, listen, mother's, often, decide, dad's, sign, quite

Unit 3 Words

spot, die, step, date, point, join, airport, woke, tooth, thankful, rode, ticket, enjoy, finish, build, library, fifty, careful, paid, wreck

Unit 4 Words

post, bedroom, lead, brave, horn, he's, meal, October, drove, space, spend, o'clock, grew, there's, awhile, I've, orange, kitchen, twelve, surprise

Unit 5 Words

wheel, sport, past, north, brick, cost, purple, seal, tiny, fur, ahead, circle, movie, present, worm, death, month, saddle, barrel, coffee

Unit 6 Words

pot, wolf, midnight, dig, ocean, alone, hotel, trick, treat, size, weather, ghost, drew, upstairs, agent, Halloween, witch, follow, plain, though

Unit 7 Words

gold, kid, bill, awake, ant, goat, short, shore, pass, half, playground, felt, bowl, moss, family, answer, cheese, telephone, America, women

Unit 9 Words

case, page, oil, slip, nail, fix, November, noon, daylight, break, desert, wagon, pound, ready, isn't, bare, led, eighteen, through, threw

Unit 10 Words

grandfather, grandmother, age, inch, grandpa, grandma, math, penny, God, coin, turkey, beg, noise, company, Thanksgiving, either, stood, angel, evening, whose

Unit 11 Words

asleep, without, become, dive, bake, hook, reach, fence, brush, dead, real, holiday, program, nearly, roll, tight, laugh, trouble, enough, microscope

Unit 12 Words

fit, wall, rainy, gum, row, December, hung, pack, stock, amount, nobody, phone, slept, candle, bloom, somewhere, wore, together, reindeer, sleigh

Unit 13 Words

rice, slow, list, cast, ruler, free, true, suit, held, track, eve, loose, voice, brother's, easy, won't, busy, between, shoot, minute

Unit 14 Words

belong	hurry
driver	maybe
butter	bottom
sack	earth
nurse	famous
shirt	early
mind	planet
farmer	cotton
base	you'll
dirty	bullet

Unit 15 Words

drank	sleepy
luck	sunny
tip	mostly
beside	silver
mice	valley
seem	woman
twenty	sight
silk	coal
mess	engine
teeth	toward

Unit 16 Words

cover	nothing
spoke	everywhere
east	scare
state	everyone
slid	haven't
arrow	poem
sweet	during
spoon	worry
shoe	doctor
rocket	sudden

Unit 17 Words

spent	bite
west	spread
rang	clothing
report	pocket
forgive	chase
crash	police
beach	pants
fort	January
hang	remember
dug	February

Unit 19 Words

mouth	star
glass	stairs
sharp	wrong
care	monkey
study	raise
tear	pear
bow	fairy
yard	button
yesterday	thirty
soft	marry

Unit 20 Words

jet	able
March	health
cab	gym
sad	sugar
finger	young
bush	magic
cool	middle
thousand	couldn't
highway	reason
wooden	league

Unit 21 Words

crown	war
trap	draw
forgot	beat
sold	load
note	breakfast
fireplace	fresh
taken	freeze
cross	hungry
tie	catcher
snake	believe

Unit 22 Words

lawn	sir
plan	somebody
map	blew
smoke	corner
ranch	Mister
seven	cause
sore	different
cloth	board
sale	fourth
tail	tomorrow

Unit 23 Words

queen	self
dust	leaves
shape	happen
rule	picnic
zoo	attack
wife	quick
peas	quiet
everything	field
climb	mighty
wheat	business

Unit 24 Words

cave	share
shell	April
smell	anybody
save	captain
wire	sure
deer	wouldn't
sock	fifteen
airplane	secret
wonder	instead
club	diamond

Unit 25 Words

May	flew
tea	forest
rich	single
newspaper	circus
jail	heart
plane	princess
trade	quit
branch	else
lamb	special
seventh	you're

Unit 26 Words

chop	heavy
heat	knee
unless	invite
honey	knife
pipe	potato
strange	Bible
shout	whistle
army	cousin
plenty	cabinet
spelling	beautiful

Unit 27 Words

pop
job
match
being
lie
crew
broken
lady
huge
himself
such
policeman
brain
oak
bubble
already
mirror
recess
August
squirrel

Unit 28 Words

feast
bunch
herself
smile
stage
enter
cattle
chew
June
feather
chick
silly
stuck
cottage
interesting
problem
act
escape
really
probably

Unit 29 Words

nap
junk
sail
till
belt
person
porch
July
spy
myself
history
hour
anyway
station
patch
vacation
hundred
sew
ankle
chocolate

Handwriting Reference Section

Unit 1 Words

grand
son
thin
life
smart
bean
seat
rather
rubber
fry
September
bottle
aren't
whole
bought
wrote
hasn't
shouldn't
mountain
certain

Unit 2 Words

less
alike
wide
alive
pay
block
dry
baseball
spider
cabin
bike
brighter
skate
listen
mother's
often
decide
dad's
sign
quite

Handwriting models in this book are from the Zaner-Bloser *Creative Growth With Handwriting* alphabet.

Unit 3 Words

spot
die
step
date
point
join
airport
woke
tooth
thankful
rode
ticket
enjoy
finish
build
library
fifty
careful
paid
wreck

Unit 4 Words

post
bedroom
lead
brave
horn
he's
meal
October
drove
space
spend
o'clock
grew
there's
awhile
I've
orange
kitchen
twelve
surprise

Unit 5 Words

wheel
sport
past
north
brick
cost
purple
seal
tiny
fur
ahead
circle
movie
present
worm
death
month
saddle
barrel
coffee

Unit 6 Words

pot
wolf
midnight
dig
ocean
alone
hotel
trick
treat
size
weather
ghost
drew
upstairs
agent
Halloween
witch
follow
plain
though

Unit 7 Words

gold
kid
bill
awake
ant
goat
short
shore
pass
half
playground
felt
bowl
moss
family
answer
cheese
telephone
America
women

Unit 9 Words

case
page
oil
slip
nail
fix
November
noon
daylight
break
desert
wagon
pound
ready
isn't
bare
led
eighteen
through
threw

Unit 10 Words

grandfather
grandmother
age
inch
grandpa
grandma
math
penny
God
coin
turkey
beg
noise
company
Thanksgiving
either
stood
angel
evening
whose

Unit 11 Words

asleep
without
become
dive
bake
hook
reach
fence
brush
dead
real
holiday
program
nearly
roll
tight
laugh
trouble
enough
microscope

Unit 12 Words

fit
wall
rainy
gum
row
December
hung
pack
stock
amount
nobody
phone
slept
candle
bloom
somewhere
wore
together
reindeer
sleigh

Unit 13 Words

rice
slow
list
cast
ruler
free
true
suit
held
track
eve
loose
voice
brother's
easy
won't
busy
between
shoot
minute

Unit 14 Words

belong
driver
butter
sack
nurse
shirt
mind
farmer
base
dirty
hurry
maybe
bottom
earth
famous
early
planet
cotton
you'll
bullet

Unit 15 Words

drank
luck
tip
beside
mice
seem
twenty
silk
mess
teeth
sleepy
sunny
mostly
silver
valley
woman
sight
coal
engine
toward

Unit 16 Words

cover
spoke
east
state
slid
arrow
sweet
spoon
shoe
rocket
nothing
everywhere
scare
everyone
haven't
poem
during
worry
doctor
sudden

Unit 17 Words

spent
west
rang
report
forgive
crash
beach
fort
hang
dug
bite
spread
clothing
pocket
chase
police
pants
January
remember
February

Unit 19 Words

mouth
glass
sharp
care
study
tear
bow
yard
yesterday
soft
star
stairs
wrong
monkey
raise
pear
fairy
button
thirty
marry

Unit 20 Words

jet
March
cab
sad
finger
bush
cool
thousand
highway
wooden
able
health
gym
sugar
young
magic
middle
couldn't
reason
league

Unit 21 Words

crown
trap
forgot
sold
note
fireplace
taken
cross
tie
snake
war
draw
beat
load
breakfast
fresh
freeze
hungry
catcher
believe

Unit 22 Words

lawn
plan
map
smoke
ranch
seven
sore
cloth
sale
tail
sir
somebody
blew
corner
Mister
cause
different
board
fourth
tomorrow

Unit 23 Words

queen
dust
shape
rule
zoo
wife
peas
everything
climb
wheat
self
leaves
happen
picnic
attack
quick
quiet
field
mighty
business

Unit 24 Words

cave
shell
smell
save
wire
deer
sock
airplane
wonder
club
share
April
anybody
captain
sure
wouldn't
fifteen
secret
instead
diamond

Unit 25 Words

May
tea
rich
newspaper
jail
plane
trade
branch
lamb
seventh
flew
forest
single
circus
heart
princess
quit
else
special
you're

Unit 26 Words

chop
heat
unless
honey
pipe
strange
shout
army
plenty
spelling
heavy
knee
invite
knife
potato
Bible
whistle
cousin
cabinet
beautiful

Unit 27 Words

pop
job
match
being
lie
crew
broken
lady
huge
himself
such
policeman
brain
oak
bubble
already
mirror
recess
August
squirrel

Unit 28 Words

feast
bunch
herself
smile
stage
enter
cattle
chew
June
feather
chick
silly
stuck
cottage
interesting
problem
act
escape
really
probably

Unit 29 Words

nap
junk
sail
till
belt
person
porch
July
spy
myself
history
hour
anyway
station
patch
vacation
hundred
sew
ankle
chocolate

Handwriting Models

A B C D E F G

H I J K L M N

O P Q R S T U

V W X Y Z

a b c d e f g

h i j k l m n

o p q r s t u

v w x y z